HEAVEN IN THE NOW

A JOURNEY THROUGH MIND, BODY & SOUL

HEAVEN IN THE NOW

A JOURNEY THROUGH MIND, BODY & SOUL

CHAD D. MCKINNEY

ONE LOVE
PUBLISHING

ONE LOVE PUBLISHING

ISBN: 978-1-7347914-2-6 (Paperback)
ISBN: 978-1-7347914-4-0 (eBook)

Library of Congress Control Number: 2021900803

Cover design by Anita Friedrich, with guidance from my Family and Ece Iraz Dinçer
Edited by Chad D. McKinney
Photography by Anita Friedrich
Reviewed by (listed alphabetically) Janel Briones, Shophar Graves, and Tony Teora
Printed by Kindle Direct Publishing, in the United States of America

One Love Publishing
San Diego, California USA
Please send all correspondence to onelovepublishinginc@gmail.com
OneLoveHolisticHealth.com

Contents

DEDICATION

All praise be to GOD. I am forever grateful for my Mom, Dad, Sister, her Husband and Son. Our Grandparents who remain, and those who have transitioned, still guiding and protecting us to this day. My uncles, aunts, cousins, and friends. All my teachers and coaches. Thanks for being with me through thick and thin. Obrigado Anjo par voce e suas Familia. Eu te Amo siempre.

Thank you to my parents for modeling unconditional Love. For encouraging us to dream big and know that we can do and be anything. For reminding us to laugh and not take things so seriously, that Life is composed of choices. For demonstrating what it means to give tirelessly of our self, without expectation of praise or recognition. For teaching us to be humble and charitable. For showing us the meaning of hard work, forgiveness, and perseverance. For believing in us. For allowing us to make our own mistakes. For having the patience and courage to know this would eventually lead to growth, stability, and fortitude. Words can never express, or do justice, as to how much we Love you. To how honored and grateful we are to have you as parents. Thank you Mom and Dad.

PREFACE

In 2006, I began a nonprofit organization when I moved to San Diego. By 2014, I lost nearly everything that I held dear. *All I ever wanted to do was help people.* Over time, the charity and my Life became indistinguishable. I followed a dream to help people living on the streets, and nearly wound up there as well. The woman I deeply Loved for three and a half years, turned down my marriage proposal and immediately moved in with someone else. Although it was largely my doing, that didn't make it any less painful. This was weeks after running for mayor and not even making the ballot. In January 2014, our charity came to a crashing halt. Years of eighty to ninety-hour work weeks, coupled with countless death threats, theft, and political corruption had finally taken a toll. I fought tooth and nail until July 2014 to reopen the doors, but by then I was broken. I couldn't even speak to a potential funder without tearing up. I was spent.

I was more than $300K in debt, and my business owed the federal government over $50K in back taxes. One morning, two IRS agents arrived unannounced at my door to discuss this further (and see what they could take from my home). My gums bled for several weeks and were beginning to fall off in pieces. This was due to stress and poor upkeep. At that time, dental insurance was the furthest thing from my mind. I was at my wits end, experiencing a nervous breakdown every couple of hours. If I finished half a bowl of oatmeal for the day, confetti should have rained from the sky. I lost nearly 30 lbs. (which is a lot on my naturally smaller frame). Hours would pass where I simply could not move. This lasted for months. I couldn't live in my van, because I already returned that to the title loan company. A last ditch effort to keep the business running a hopeful moment longer. In July 2014, I was down to nearly 115 lbs. and came to the harsh realization that it was time to take care of myself. I officially closed the doors to the charity.

In August 2014, I began my PhD in psychology. At the same time, I volunteered at my friend's bike shop to get my head right. To make this happen, I rode my bike thirty miles a day to and from work. As I focused on loving myself first, doors began to open. With school being my only real job, I had time to pour back into myself. Exercise, meditation, nutrition, and traveling were at the top of the list. In 2015, my passion for surfing brought me a Life changing idea. Initially, I didn't have enough money to pay an attorney to file the patent, so I taught myself three hundred hours of patent law and filed these myself. I contacted my Cousin, a nuclear engineer in Hawaii, to assist me with the design. Following a deep meditation in April 2016, I received an unexpected call to showcase our product on a major television show. We hit the ground running, filming our episode later that year. Our product will launch in surf shops across the United States and Australia in 2020. In February 2017, I was married on a beach in La Jolla. Although we are no longer together, I wouldn't trade that amazing experience for anything in the world. This coming summer, I will have earned my doctorate in psychology with an emphasis in teaching. Not bad for a young man expelled from high school his senior year. I offer my story in hopes that it will save others any avoidable suffering, in rediscovering the Peace that resides within each of us. Once we have touched this Peace, we are Free to create the Life of our dreams.

Virtues and references to our higher Self are capitalized throughout this book to remind us of their importance in our Life.

INTRODUCTION

After backpacking solo through Europe and Asia for a little over a year, I returned home, ready to take on the world. I stayed with my Family for a few months before moving to San Diego. A couple weeks into being back, my Dad and I got into a heated discussion regarding God. I left the house that night because I couldn't hear anymore.

Dad: So, you're telling me you don't believe in God?

Me: Not only do I not believe in God, I wish it was socially acceptable for me to tattoo the word "god" across my forehead, with a circle and a slash through it!

Dad: So, what's to prevent someone from just doing whatever they want then?

Me: Love. Themselves. Being a good person. We don't need some fake pie in the sky, Chris Cringle jingle to make us behave and treat each other with Love and Respect.

Dad: Chris Cringle?

Me: Santa Clause. You better watch out. You better not cry. It's a scam! Religion is made to control the masses. You better do what we say, or you're gonna burn in eternal hell fire when you're dead. Come on! Not only do I not believe in god, I wish I was around the very moment after people died, so that I could laugh at 'em and tell 'em they wasted their whole Life.

My Mom jumped in at that point. There are only a couple ways that conversation can go from there. My Dad never hit me growing up, but he likely should have, and repeatedly. In the process of realizing Heaven within, I was relentless in my search for Truth. Daily, I would steer conversations towards that of religion and God. The line in the sand had been drawn. The more they questioned or waned, the more I felt justified in my fight against religion, apathy, and blind faith. Years later, I understood this to be a desperate attempt to 'justify' my beliefs, by belittling those of 'others'.

To say that I was 'atheist' was no different than saying I was 'Christian' or 'Muslim'. How can any word define the undefinable? While reading this book, please consider the guidance of Mikhail Naimy. In "The Book of Mirdad", he cautioned, "words, at best, are flashes that reveal horizons; they are not the way to those horizons; still less are they those horizons."[1]

This book is intended to provide tools in understanding the formation of our reality, as well as our Power and Freedom to choose it every moment. There is a direct, indisputable correlation between reality (often exemplified as Health) and perception. Bear in mind, Health is a holistic endeavor. For example, if our physical health improves, so it is with our mental, emotional, and sexual health. As the saying goes, a rising tide raises all ships. Throughout this book, options for improving our mental, physical, emotional, spiritual, and sexual Health are provided. Most importantly, this book provides resources and insights for tapping into the Peace that resides within each of us. It is from here, that Heaven is revealed.

~ One LOVE. One GOD

HEAVEN IN THE NOW

A JOURNEY THROUGH MIND, BODY & SOUL

A HOLY CONVERGENCE

HEAVEN

"Heaven is not a place you go to. It is a place you grow to."

- Edgar Cayce[2]

Religion has given Heaven a bad name. Many good-hearted people have a hard time swallowing the contradictions and prejudices embedded in popular religious texts. The predominant religion of a nation is that chosen by its conquerors.[3] From modern-day crusades to holy wars, it's easy to see how people become disenchanted with religions gaining converts through exploitive, imperialistic means. Indigenous beliefs eventually fall relic, lost to generational amnesia. When children express innocent curiosity and constructive thought, they are often berated or talked over. Those on a genuine quest for Truth, are socially and systematically ostracized.

Indoctrinated and confused, I associated GOD with religion. Repulsed at the thought of treating this Life like a waiting room, I pillaged doubt with a ferocity that would make the Crusades look like a suggestion:

∞ If everything stems from Creation, then who created God? Who is God's God?

∞ If God is so loving, all-knowing, and forgiving; then why do we have war and famine? Why do the innocent suffer?

∞ The concept of God and the afterlife is a coping mechanism to deal with the fear and deep-down certainty that one day we will die. We live. We die. That's it. What happens in between is up to us.

Of note, the purpose of this book is not to bash or dismantle religion. Science and spirituality are not in competition. My friend summed it up well, "all of us are just trying to find Peace". This Peace is already within us, we've simply been conditioned to forget. Our egos blind us with an illusion that we are in some way disconnected from GOD. That Existence is in any way separable. To break the confines of past conditionings and enter a state of tangible Prayer (commune), I have found it helpful to understand GOD, The Oneness, as a verb. Again, all words fall short. Understanding this requires a deep look into the constructs of perception and its reality. As we peel back layers of the onion, our Peace is revealed. Herein lies our Heaven.

DYING AS AN INFINITE BEING

"To Learn to die is to be liberated from it."

~ Bruce Lee[4]

Facing Death

In the Shawshank Redemption, after spending the last two months isolated in the hole, Andy Dufrain (Tim Robbins) reemerges into general custody. Speaking as if diagnosed with a terminal illness, Andy shares where he'll go and what he'll do, if he gets out of prison. Red (Morgan Freeman) becomes uncomfortable, consoling Andy as best he can. "I don't think you oughta be doing this to yourself Andy. Those are just shitty pipe dreams! I mean, Mexico is way the hell down there, and you're in here. And that's just the way it is!" Andy muscles his words through the tightening of his throat, "I guess it comes down to a simple choice really. Get busy living. Or, get busy dying."

We could die at any moment. The same could be said to live. Ironically, it was death that converted me to atheism, and it was death that opened my eyes to God. At twenty, my close Friend lost his younger Sister in a car accident. It was at that moment, I denounced my Faith in God. I had enough. There was no justification fathomable to explain their suffering.

I decided then and there to choose quality over quantity. Longevity and the promise of tomorrow had lost all appeal. My first meditation with death occurred long before I knew what meditation was. After breaking my jaw in sparring, I instinctively turned to the mirror. I knew I was going to backpack 'Europe' and 'Asia'. I had no idea what I was chasing, but the bet was waged, and I laid my Soul upon the table. I was willing to put it all on the line, even if that meant dying. My Parents eventually realized they weren't going to change my mind. My Dad, knowing of my stubbornness, wanted to reassure me. "Now Son, you know if things ever get too bad, you can always come back early. You don't have to stay a whole year." I had a thousand dollars in my pocket and was willing to eat garbage and sleep in bushes. "Thanks Dad, but the only way I'm coming back before a year, is in a body bag." There were plenty of opportunities for that.

Looking in the mirror, I knew I had a chance of dying. I knew death was real. I understood that even young people can die. My pupils stormed the outer edge of my irises. My Soul swallowed the borders. Tears slowly streamed down my cheeks. I had accepted my mortality, as an atheist. There was no tomorrow in this acquiescence. This was game over. You did your best. Thanks for playing. I was Free…

Near Death & Out of Body Experiences

"The Kingdom of GOD is within man! Not one man, nor a group of men, but in all men! All men are Created equal!"

- Charlie Chaplin in "The Great Dictator" referencing the seventh chapter of St. Luke in the New Testament.[5]

I don't remember the exact year, but sometime around 2008 I nearly died on a snowboarding trip to upper Wisconsin. What occurred is known as a near death and out of body experience. People all over the planet, across all denominations, have reported similar NDE and OBEs. Themes include being immersed in the Light, review of one's Life, communication with a higher being, meeting God, receiving a message, and an altered Life path from that day forth.[6] Researching these further, may help in easing the pain of ever losing a Loved one, or any lingering fear regarding our own eventual passing.

I nearly died, and I deserved to. While on the chairlift, my Friends and I saw someone sliding down the mountain on their butt. *Let's snowplow her!* One Friend wasn't for it. The other, "yea! I'll trail and we'll get her twice!" We bombed the run. I was roaring at least 30 mph down the mountain. First off, we should never snowplow any stranger, let alone a woman. As I approached, I saw that she was not even a woman, but a young girl. I wanted to go right by her. She was way too young and had no business getting snowplowed. I still have the feeling of being a real asshole even typing this to be Honest with you. Ego kicked in. *Na, my Friends need to know I'm still the same me. I'm still crazy and fun and don't give a ----. Maybe I'll just kick a little snow.* As I approached, I saw her eyes widen in terror. *God I'm so sorry for what I did here.* Out of being an asshole, I kicked a little snow on her legs doing 30 mph. The trail doglegged left, and going that speed, I didn't plan for it. Straight in front of me, was a cliff leading to a forest of towering oak trees. If I was on the ground, I couldn't walk a straight line through those bowling pins. The only gutter was my mind.

Just before hitting the first tree, I left my body and was asked, "Now?" *"No, not yet. I still have too much I have to do here."* The question and answer occurred simultaneously. All that existed in this moment was Peace and Love. My Friends tell me they saw me bounce off the trees like a pinball. Flipping one direction, bouncing up from the giant drop off, hitting another tree, and then spinning a completely different direction. I didn't feel a thing until I rejoined my body. Thank God I had my helmet. Before my Friends arrived, they thought for sure I was dead. As I lifted my face from the snow, I felt tons of liquid pouring from my nose. I figured I had broken my nose and shattered my face. I didn't know or care what had happened. I was overwhelmed with such Joy and Appreciation to be alive! I couldn't believe it! *I'm alive!!! Hahah!! I'm alive!!* I repeated this a thousand times the next two days! The liquid pouring from my nose was only water. I had, at most, two scratches across my cheek. Not even deep cuts. That's it! I later came to understand that we are all offered opportunities in this Life, on this plane of existence, to "opt out". Basically, hit the reset button and begin again. New body. New Life. New opportunities.

Past and Future Lives are Real

As a child, James Leininger had an affinity for planes. At three, his obsession and knowledge of aircrafts made his Parents take notice. As his verbal communication skills improved, he would describe the mechanical parts of a plane. He was also able to recall locations in the South Pacific where the naval aircraft carriers were stationed during the war, and even specific names of the planes. This information would only be privy to historians, or those in the military. James informed his Parents that his plane crashed after being hit by the 'Japanese'. Investigation into this phenomenon revealed that James was reciting the Life of James M. Huston, Jr. Bear in mind, James was still only around three years old at the time. Later he met the surviving Family of Mr. Huston, Jr., who are also convinced this young man is the reincarnated fallen soldier.[7] This is just one, of thousands of examples, of individuals recalling past lives. For more information regarding past lives, and our ability to access a greater spectrum of Consciousness, I recommend further researching Edgar Cayce (1877 – 1945). Discussed shortly in the section examining Consciousness.

Do We Need to Die in Order to Live?

L ife is often hardest on the living. When a Loved one transitions, it is for us whom we weep. We miss them. We look back on what was, and what could've been. So much of our Life is controlled by a fear of death. Operating under the illusion that we will somehow live forever in this form. These bodies are just leased vehicles for our Consciousness to travel through. We return them to the Earth when it's time to move on. Life continues after Life, as death is an illusion.

Often people remember the value of Life, while lying on their death bed. Old age and 'terminal illness' force a new perspective upon weary eyes. Suddenly it is easy to find Joy in the 'little' things. The sights, sounds, smells, touches, tastes, feelings...

However, we need not be diagnosed with a terminal illness to Appreciate Life. The practice of feeling that our time is limited encourages us to stop living for tomorrow. Rushing to get 'somewhere' else. Meddling in the mundane and scrutinizing the trivial. All we ever have is Here and Now, and this is perfect. Appreciation is the key that opens the door to Heaven. LOVE walks us through.

Let's Get Honest with Our Self

In Her TEDx Talk, Kalina Silverman, detailed two questions she would ask strangers to skip the small talk.[8] The results were profound. I believe asking ourselves these same questions, will help break down barriers, and get to what really matters in our Life. Go ahead and write the answers:

1. What do I want to do before I die?

    _____

    _____

    _____

    _____

    _____

2. If I knew I was going to die tomorrow, what would I do?

    _____

    _____

    _____

    _____

    _____

> Appreciation is the key that
>
> opens the door to Heaven.
>
> **LOVE walks Us through.**

PERCEPTION & ITS REALITY

The Formations of Perception

It's easy to look with just our eyes and be blinded. Since birth, our perception has been held hostage. Constructed, distracted, and skewed. Misled into bigotry and blame. Hampered by divisiveness, trapped by greed, and pulled into vanity's abyss. How painful it is to interact with this world through an imaginary ego. Turning away from an Ever-Present, Divine Guidance. Dr. Barbara Brennan diagnoses all human suffering to stem from the illusion of separation.[9]

How does separation occur? Can ears or the physical eyes discriminate? No. This occurs in the mind. Mind, meaning ego here. A set of beliefs incorporated and practiced through indoctrination. These thoughts, feelings, beliefs, and even behaviors are then identified as a 'me'. The ego is conditioned to perceive the world as composed of 'me' and 'others'. 'Good', 'bad', 'right', and 'wrong'. Life is then strained through the mind, and interpreted by a fabricated identity.

It's said that "we see things not as they are, but as we are." This really sucks to hear and think at first. However, letting go of our attachment to how we view ourselves, and/or want to be viewed, it's one of Life's most beautiful realizations. Surrender takes Courage. It is the ultimate expression of Strength and Humility.

So how do we view Life beyond ego? By knowing the difference between looking and Witnessing, we bypass our conditioning. Looking is an active process of trying to make sense of what is being seen through a previously assembled worldview. Witnessing is Observing without judgment or expectation. Involved, yet unattached. Pure Witnessing is one with the moment, Free of past and future. There is no face to Witnessing. When we move without thought, from the Silence of our being; we realize Peace.

There is no face to

Witnessing.

Drunk on Expectations

A group of participants were given access to nonalcoholic beer, and informed that the researchers wanted to assess the effects of alcohol on group dynamics. These individuals were then placed in a room with a keg and told to mingle. Shortly after, people were behaving as if intoxicated. Voices raised, speech slurred, balance kilted, and a few even vomited. Others began hooking up. C. Wright Mills summed it up best, "if a person perceives a situation as real, it is real in its consequence."

My Iiiiiii's!

One afternoon I was harassing my Sister as she got ready to leave the house. Before I could blink my eyes, she grabbed a nearby bottle and sprayed me in the face. I looked down at the yellow packaging, "hair detangler". There might as well have been a skull and crossbones on the bottle. Before my sight was stricken, I mustered all my strength to look her in the face one more time. She was smiling ear to ear. I dropped to me knees, "My eyes!!! You----! I'm blind!!! Ahhhhh!!!" My Dad stomped and roared down the hall. "What the hell's going on in here?!" She'd never looked so happy and disgusted all at the same time. "It's water." I slowly blinked the humiliation out of my eyes (as best I could).

Focus

"What you focus on, you feel."

- Tony Robbins[10]

A s I began opening my eyes to the injustices of the world, I was at no loss for confirmation. Seek and we shall find. Educational, religious, political, corporate, and media interests utilize classical and operant conditioning methodology (discussed in the following chapter), and control of resources, to train individual consciousness to serve their own agenda. This can take many a form, and the results are dreadful. For example, poor school systems, unstable or abusive households, sexual repression, criminal activity in the community, a privatized prison system, religious indoctrination, the illusion of race, bigotry, corrupt cops, fictional financial systems, delusive elections, and/or war. Just to name a few.

In the pursuit of Justice, I scoured the Earth searching for the source of these abominations. The more I found, the angrier I became. Although my intentions were to help, anger was still the vibration and frequency I was tuning into.

We are the radios, and 'reality' the stations. All channels lay dormant right now at our beck and call. Our radio will play what we tune it to. As our Consciousness continues to expand, if we ignore this responsibility, we'll end up listening to a lot of static. Our micro Universe is the result of our moment to moment vibration. Our choices, thoughts, feelings, and perception influence its frequency. As Shantam Nityama says, "Energy follows thought. Always."[11] Joy attracts bliss, while Gratitude begets Appreciation. This can be Witnessed in the experiences that unfold in our daily Life. It is our choice what we choose to **focus** on.

Training Opportunities

For example, take something as simple as walking down the street to an appointment. Let's say we're still ruminating over a conflict that happened five minutes ago. Whatever the circumstance, does this sound familiar:

That son of a ---!

I can't believe he said I was ---!

Next time I see him…

My vibration lowers with every negative remark. Anger brings the blood to a boil. Lost in thought, I pass a 'stranger' on the street and receive a look that would stop a bus. *What's **their** problem?!* Just then someone bumps into me. No sorry. No nothing. They're already on their way. Wondering if I should chase them down and demand an apology, I miss the crosswalk. I arrive at my appointment only to be informed that I'm late and will need to reschedule. A callous clerk just purchased a first-class ticket on the pain train. *Woooo! Woooo! All aboard!!*

Now, although we cannot step in the same river twice, let's say I'm walking down that same street so to speak. Same situation leading up

15

to it. However, this time, Gratitude is pouring in. "I can't believe that person said that! Whew. Hahah. Well, that's just where they are for the moment. Much Love to 'em. Probably won't be calling anytime soon." I then **focus** on Gratitude. "What a blessing to be alive. God this air feels so fresh and vibrant. My legs feel strong. I never noticed the rhythm of my walk before. Each step sounds like a note to a symphony. Even the traffic has a music to it. I'm so Grateful that I have ears to hear this…" Here, the incident was acknowledged, but not dwelled upon. We can train our Self to focus on the positive, until this becomes a reflex.

Our radio will play

what we tune it to.

Conditioning Processes

*Warning! *The remainder of this chapter may feel like we're doing homework. However, it's necessary. The following principles are a Powerful influence upon individual and group 'reality'. We can either use these to our benefit, or be used by them for someone else's.*

The formation and execution of most daily behavior is the result of conditioning. Therefore, prior to examining reality, it's important to first understand the constructs influencing our perception and choices. For these guide behavior. In the field of psychology, this can be traced to the processes of classical and operant conditioning. Once we have gained an understanding of these foundational principles, we will consider how they are exerted upon our reality through the use of symbols, framing, and labels. After that, it's back to the fun stuff.

Classical Conditioning

In the early twentieth century, Ivan Pavlov discovered that dogs will unintentionally salivate when presented with food. The salivation is an involuntary response. Meaning, the dogs do not think, "cool, now it's time to produce saliva so I can chow down." Saliva is the body's way of preparing the stomach for the process of digestion. Whenever food was presented, a bell was rung. Signifying the arrival of food. Here, the bell is the neutral stimulus. Pavlov discovered that over time, the dogs would still salivate, even when only presented with the bell. In essence, ringing a bell produced the same result as if delivering food to the canines. However, if the bell was rung, but not accompanied with food for an extended period of time, eventually the dogs ceased producing saliva in preparation of digestion. They no longer expected food. The association was broken.

Operant Conditioning

Operant conditioning was developed by B. F. Skinner in 1938. Operant conditioning is the cultivation of 'voluntary' behavior (whereas a dog salivating is an involuntary, biological response). Behavior is directed then learned through correlation. For simplicity, a behavior is performed (not performed), it is rewarded or punished. The individual then behaves in accordance to their understanding of this association. For example, an individual will refrain from speeding to avoid a negative punishment (the loss of money or one's freedom). Whereas, another person will punch a clock in order to receive a paycheck to meet one's basic needs. This is regarded as a positive reinforcement.

Real Consequences

In a token economy, an individual is given a token (reward) when completing a task. The token(s) can then be used to obtain goods or services. Say, washing dishes to earn money to purchase food from the grocery store. A token economy works when individuals have Faith that the token is necessary to obtain the desired items or services. The token is therefore believed to be valuable. **This principle is an exact replica perpetuating and sustaining every single economic system across this planet.** When these tokens ('money') are printed out of thin air, or simply typed into a database; how is there no money for food, shelter, health care, education, et cetera, but there is 'money' for wars and defense budgets of conquest proportions?

Questions:

1. In what ways are our thoughts and behaviors the result of classical conditioning?

    _____

    _____

    _____

    _____

2. How have our thoughts and behaviors been directed through operant conditioning?

    _____

    _____

    _____

    _____

3. Are token economies necessary at this stage of human evolution? Why, or why not?

    _____

    _____

    _____

    _____

The Use of Symbols

What word(s) does this symbol represent?

Now, what word(s) does this image symbolize?

Both images are meant to invoke a feeling. Even though each image represents a 'heart', one feels more ethereal or even cartoonish, whereas the other feels more grounded in 'reality'. The first may even be regarded as a symbol of Love. Why is that? How can different images represent the same word, or even multiple words? How can the same word have a different feeling when represented by various images/symbols?

Culture, ambition, and personal experience will influence the degree and type of feeling elicited. So when Colin Kaepernick kneels during the 'national' anthem, he is bringing attention, and refusing to pay homage to, a corrupt system that since its inception has oppressed and murdered people with dark skin. When a veteran removes their cap and places a hand over their heart, they are doing so in Honor of thoughts associated with bravery, Courage, Respect, dignity, equality, and Freedom. How can two behaviors be so diametrically different?

The cloth and the song remained the same. Both associations boil down to choice. Empathy results when we step outside of our worldview, and try to put ourselves in another's shoes for a moment. We gain Understanding through Openness.

Framing

If behavior results from conditioning, how is perception formed? Quickly after birth, worldviews are contorted to fit someone else's agenda. Framing is the presentation of information in either a positive or negative context. This can include, text, audio, and/or graphics paired with a message instigating a desired response from the recipient. This can be dangerous when in the hands of political lobbyists or marketers. Individuals and groups of people can be swayed to contribute to a cause without understanding the breadth of their well-intentioned decision. This is first accomplished by presenting the illusion that the individual has only one of two choices. Second, the information is loaded to stimulate emotion and manipulate thoughts. Third, the individual or group, behave in accordance with the intention of the message and messenger.

An Example

In the 1960's, the invasion of Vietnam was originally presented as a war for 'democracy'. Many during the Civil Rights Movement saw through this hoax. This included everyone from the Panthers caring for their communities, to the college campuses proposing a general strike. The Hippies, Yippies, and Weathermen also played their part. Yet, people were still willing to be drafted, travel to a foreign land, and kill for something they were told to believe in. However, this changed when the **presentation** regarding the purpose and effects of the war changed. When the rampant carpet bombings and loss of innocent Life were brought to Light, public outcry reached a fever pitch. After it became evident that this was nothing more than another war for oil, the momentum shifted and U.S. troops began returning home.

The Power of Labels

Cognitive framing is the interpretation of stimuli to either one's benefit or detriment. However, this would be of little effect without the use of labels. In the government and media, military invasions on foreign soil are deemed 'wars'. Often wars for something, such as: Freedom, democracy, national security, or defense. People fighting for the 'winning' team are dubbed 'soldiers'. Human beings on the 'opposing' side are demarked 'terrorists' or 'insurgents'. The death of innocent women, men, and children in a military conflict is referred to as 'collateral damage' by the invaders. While this same human loss is incited as 'murder', and/or an act of 'cowardice' and 'terrorism' by those on the defensive. Labels are used to divide and conquer. Pitting group 'A' v. group 'B', who may or may not be allies with group 'C'.

Labels are a subtle means of controlling behavior. It is human nature to want to be accepted by the in-group. When someone participates in accordance with a particular agenda, they are deemed 'good', 'just', or 'right'. Their desire for social belonging is fulfilled. Opposition receives a less favorable demarcation and consequence. *Operant conditioning at its finest.* Now this is where things get interesting. 'Countries' and 'religions' have histories and missions (agendas). This requires 'allies', 'enemies', 'leaders', 'followers', and/or 'soldiers'.

Accepting an identity through acquiescence to a label, we embody an alleged history, and willfully perpetuate someone else's story. *It's only after we have labeled something as beautiful, that it becomes totally ugly.*

Question:

1. *What labels have we believed about our Self that may serve to divide us from others?*

_____

_____

_____

_____

Understanding Our Power in Labeling

As mentioned, framing has been used to manipulate good-hearted people into making or allowing decisions that are in direct opposition to their moral compass. However, this same mechanism can also serve as a benefit to the practitioner. For example, people who are depressed are more likely to seek help when it is regarded as a sign of Strength. Individuals demonstrate greater aptitude in completing complex tasks, when errors are considered a necessary part of learning and growing. Mountains are hills. Dreams are real. The marines have a saying, "pain is just weakness leaving the body." This is a perfect example of framing. Perceiving pain and difficulties in such a manner, frames every experience, positive or negative, in a positive Light. This is an elixir to greatness. It is that extra push, when we have nothing left.

The aforementioned conditioning processes have been addressed in great detail so that we may not only recognize their influence throughout our day, but to remind us of our Power in creating our Life. Anything can be used to train our perception and hone our vibration. Choosing our thoughts affects our feelings, thereby impacting our experience. Our experience then becomes our reality. The 'meaning of Life' is found when we attribute meaning to it.[12] It is ours, and ours alone, to Create. It is an intrinsic drive, not a response to an external pressure.[13] In raising our vibration, associations can be used to remind us of our extension and expression of Divinity. That in our natural state, beyond image, time, and space; we are Peace. Eternal Consciousness having a momentary human experience.

Daily Practices

Our daily Life offers Infinite opportunities to condition our Consciousness to bring us back to our Divinity. The people of Kemet (ancient Egypt) incorporated the following technique in remembering their Divinity.[14] Anything can be conjured and used as a symbol. Have fun and be Creative:

1. Choose an object or symbol (visual and/or auditory).

   a. Anything will work. For instance, a green light, tree, glass of water, car horn, the number 22, or a hummingbird.

2. Choose a meaning for this object or symbol.

   a. For instance, a sign of being in alignment with our Higher Self.

3. Breathe Appreciation each time this shows up, reminding us that we are extensions and expressions of GOD.

4. It's that simple. As momentum builds, synchronicity (the overlap of events with Divine precision) increases to the point that it almost becomes expected (while still Appreciating its every occurrence).

What is Reality?

"Reality is merely an illusion, albeit a very persistent one."

- Albert Einstein[15]

Remember the power of labeling? Somewhere along the way, the insecurities of 'others', became beliefs about ourselves. We've all had moments when passion drowned out doubt and flooded fear. When we were about to take that chance and try something new. Be someone new. Then we started reading from the script someone else wrote… *This is crazy. What am I doing? When have I ever done anything like this, and what in the world makes me think I can do it now? What if…*

Life is filled with "what if's". In fact, Life is one big, continuous "what if?". We've just been led to believe the "what ifs" of 'others', are more secure than our own "what ifs". Relationships end, jobs close, economies crash, and governments are overthrown. Every year, 'nations' shake up the etch and sketch and draw new lines in the sand. What makes the "what ifs" of these entities, any more certain than our "what ifs"? Often our need for approval has us living in acquiescence to the expectations of 'others'. *At least a surrogate is paid for the use of their Womb.*

So, what is 'realistic'? It may be helpful to first ask, "What is 'reality'?" It has been suggested that the Greek philosopher, Democritus, was the first to posit the constructs of Existence as reducible to the atom (interesting that atom and Adam are near identical phonetically). Centuries later, the atom was found reducible to an electron, neutron, and proton. After which came quarks. Each stage of discovery postulating that it had uncovered the building blocks of the Universe, the basis for all matter. Propagating the Universe to be solid and static, with time and space operating as continual, unavoidable constructs.

Albert Einstein's theory of relativity suggested space-time to be dependent upon the observer's subjectivity. This countered Newtonian physics which alleged that the Universe was reducible to a physical and mechanical measurement. Then came quantum physics. The scientific discovery that socked 'realism' in the gut, then gave it a wedgie. Research in the field of quantum physics has demonstrated that 'reality' is composed of a 'wave particle'. This wave particle remains in a state of flux, until influenced by an observer. At which time, the wave bends and forms a momentary particle. Some particles affecting other particles regardless of the supposed distance between the two. Ever think of someone right when they were calling?

'Reality', is Energy that is in a state of constant flux until directed and made tangible by the influence of an Observer.

What is Consciousness?

"There is a Power with which we are Conscious."

- Vitvan[16]

If reality is in a state of flux, what does that say about Consciousness and the Observer? Consciousness has been described as an iceberg floating in the ocean. The portion which most humans are conscious of, is the tip of the iceberg. That within the nearest proximity to our immediate and most basic needs. The subconscious, is the iceberg just below view, submerged beneath the sea. The Super Conscious is the ocean and everything included in it.[17] The concept of the Super Conscious stems well-beyond what Freud had originally proposed with his theory of the id, ego, and super ego.

This is a multidimensional Universe, and we are interdimensional beings. Everything at this very moment is readily available to us, including Heaven. Michael Talbot has likened reality to that of a hologram. A hologram produces a three-dimensional image when lasers (Light) interact in a particular pattern with its photographic plate. The image(s) were always present on this plate, just not readily available to our vision in this spectrum of Light. What else is available just beyond waking Life?

Lucid Dreaming

We have been led to believe that Consciousness only exists when we are awake. Meaning that our brain, and therefore consciousness, shuts off while we are sleeping. How then do we account for lucid dreaming? Lucid dreaming is known as the ability to control one's dreams. In essence, cognitively functioning as if fully awake while sleeping. The experience of dreaming even has a direct impact on the physiological processes of the individual. Hence, the reason an individual may wake up in a cold sweat after a nightmare, or a puddle of Love after a sexual encounter. Many scientists have used this information to further substantiate the claims of Consciousness being the result of neurological activity. Basically, existing in, and only in, the brain. For those interested in Consciously navigating the dream world, the attached reference is an excellent place to start.[18]

Akashic Records

Dismissing the dream world to a neurological phenomenon appears logical, however, does not account for individuals accessing the Akashic records through altered states of Consciousness. This includes, but is not limited to, dreaming, hypnosis, meditation, and entheogenic experiences (peyote, LSD, DMT, mushrooms, ayahuasca, etc.). There are numerous individuals who have tapped into this innate ability which resides within all of us. However, Edgar Cayce is the most documented in modern, human history. He was dubbed the 'sleeping prophet', for his ability to gain access to the Akashic records through a self-induced hypnotic state. Once functioning from this expanded Self, he was asked questions by people seeking answers in their lives. The questions ranged from past lives, curing mental and physiological ailments, relationships, Atlantis, Kemet (ancient Egypt), and well beyond. Over 14,000 of these psychic readings are transcribed and available through the Association for Research and Enlightenment (A.R.E.). These are accessible online (for a small donation to keep the facility running), or at their headquarters in Virginia. Thousands of healings occurred as a result of Edgar Cayce's readings. It should be strongly noted that Mr. Cayce did not finish school past the 9th grade. However, while in his trans like state, the vocabulary often used, would be that only available to a physician or surgeon with years of experience. As most of his readings were transcribed, these would later be fact checked with medical professionals to investigate and ensure their accuracy.

Remote Viewing

Remote viewing is the perception of people, places, and events outside of one's body and immediate surroundings. Remote viewing is not limited by time, space, or even dimension. Remote viewing is more common than the media and school textbooks have led us to believe. Although there are those born with a propensity, like lucid dreaming, this is a learnable skill. Remote viewing is often discarded as 'pseudoscience', by people with no experience of the event. Usually these labels are just an attempt to protect a well-developed worldview. Remote viewing has not only been scientifically investigated, it has even been used for military purposes by the United States, Russia (Soviet Union), and China to name a few.[19] "Psychic Warrior" by David Morehouse provides an excellent read, and greater insight into this phenomenon for those interested in learning more.

Multiple Consciousness in One Body

Individuals diagnosed with dissociative identity 'disorder' (formerly known as multiple personality disorder), will often demonstrate two or more distinct personalities. Sometimes, even in the same sitting. The split of personality is commonly triggered by a traumatic event in which the individual disassociates from the experience in order to survive. For instance, sexual abuse at an early age. The experience is too much, and so the individual separates from the event, leaving their body behind. These personalities can be as distinct as night and day. This includes, but is not limited by: accents, use of language, facial expressions, body posture, personal histories, and so on. At first glance, this appears like the individual may simply be a great actor lacking critical acclaim. However, individuals diagnosed with dissociative identity disorder have also been known to demonstrate different EEG readings, heartbeats, physical gifts, varying malady, and even eye color![20] Eye color! Think about this. An individual reporting that a personality has commandeered control of her or his body in this realm, has changed their eye color!

It appears consciousness and ability are even transferable through the organs. For example, individuals receiving organ donations have been reported to have taken on, not only some of the personality traits of the donor, but even some of her or his talents or gifts.[21] For example, while recovering from an organ transplant, never previously demonstrating a smidgen of artistic ability, individuals are now painting portraits that would have Picasso questioning his choice of vocation. Parallels have also included alterations in preference towards: food, music, art, sex, recreation, and career.[22]

Expanded Consciousness

Some individuals appear to be born with a greater access into the Super Conscious. For example, Scott Flansburg, renowned as the 'Human Calculator', has demonstrated an ability to solve complex mathematical problems faster than a lecture hall filled with mathematicians armed with advanced scientific calculators.[23] Scott is not alone in his gifts. While Mr. Flansburg has been born with these gifts, it appears others are given a little push. Individuals experiencing this phenomena have been dubbed, 'accidental savants'.[24] This has been referred to as 'acquired savant syndrome'. For instance, after surviving a brain trauma resulting from a violent attack, Jason Padgett found his entire world altered. Previously only concerned with lifting weights and partying, he now could see mathematical equations in nearly every object and minute detail of his environment. The geometry he saw hidden and reflected in his everyday Life, was providing mathematical insight into the workings of the Universe. For example, how the Fibonacci code can be traced to all expressions of nature.

Savants and Geniuses

A genius savant is an individual with an uncanny mastery in a given field or subject. Often, the ability remained dormant from birth until an outside event unearthed its discovery. For instance, in a matter of minutes, Alonzo Clemens, sculpts animal figurines out of clay. Accurately depicting details that would remain veiled to the untrained eye. When asked how he is able to fashion such realism, he responded that he remembers and sees a picture in his head. The interviewer inquired where the picture came from. The Light in his eyes could serve as a beacon for ships lost at sea. Mr. Clemens replied, "God puts the picture in my head".[25]

In the same documentary, Morley Safer interviewed George Finn, a human calendar, who can provide the date if given the day, or give the day if given the date, for any point in time! When asked, Mr. Finn is also able to recall the weather and day of the week at any second of his Conscious Life. He concluded the interview by thanking Mr. Safer, "I will remember this day for the rest of my Life".

Lesley Lemke has the ability to play any musical piece after hearing it once, regardless of the length. Mr. Lemke had an uphill battle since birth. He was born blind and with cerebral. He did not walk until ten, and only began talking in his late twenties. At six months old, his foster Mother, May Lemke (an absolute Angel), placed a piano in his room and would strike the keys one at a time. When asked why she did this, she responded, "I maybe thought that I could stir something in the poor, blind boy that was laying there." Around a week later, in the middle of the night, Mr. Lemke dragged himself to the piano and began playing beautifully. Today, he fills concert halls throughout Wisconsin.

All of these examples suggest a non-localization of Consciousness. These findings, along with what we have already learned from past lives, as well as near death and out of body experiences, beckon several questions. For instance, what is the personality, and how dependent is our physiological functioning on it? So often our reality appears to be tied to a personality. This includes everything from DNA to worldviews. However, understanding these few simple concepts we must now ask ourselves, "what is our level of influence and responsibility in the construction (or realization) of this reality?"

Can We Control Reality?

In essence, 'reality' is what we make of it. Mind and body are one. Just different expressions of the same phenomenon. Mind is simply a subtler form of the same Energy, which is also expressed as body. This is how thoughts not only influence reality, but also the human body. In the field of psychology, we learn that our Health can be significantly impacted by our thoughts, feelings, intentions, and expectations.

Placeboes and Noceboes

For example, if we have Faith in a particular modality of medicine (i.e. pill, injection, cream, ointment, therapy, surgery, and so on), and we perceive the medical practitioner (doctor, psychiatrist, physician, Shaman, et cetera) as competent and credible; we are likely to experience a positive outcome to the treatment. This is known as the placebo effect. Commonly, people are given a sugar pill under the pretense that they are actually ingesting a medicine designed to meet their expectations. For example, the treatment of a malady, or enhancement of a trait (more focus, greater creativity, increased strength, improved stamina, and so on). Remarkably, placebos have demonstrated success rates as great as pharmacology in treating chemical and emotional distress, such as depression, with way less side effects.[26]

On the contrary, if a patient has a negative expectancy regarding treatment, or if the medical professional conveys the same, the individual is likely to suffer a detrimental outcome as a result of the intervention. This is known as the nocebo effect, and it can be fatal when diagnosing or treating a preconceived 'terminal' illness. Ever wonder why a person goes into the clinic for a routine checkup, receives a diagnosis that scares the Life out of them, then dies two weeks later? The wealth of research demonstrating the potential for a placebo or nocebo effect to occur, serves as a call to compel the American Medical Association to take a much needed look into their current code of medical ethics.

We get it, the power of mind, right? That's fine and dandy with a common cold, but what about when things get serious and I need surgery? Interestingly, placebo surgeries have demonstrated success similar to the 'real deal', in treating maladies such as Alzheimer's, Parkinson's, osteoporotic vertebral fractures, severe asthma, coronary issues, obesity, sleep apnoea, and a myriad of others.[27] As the patient perceives the severity of the situation to be escalated through the use of surgery, therefore of greater importance, placebo surgeries have demonstrated a greater success rate, than mere ingestion of a placebic.[28]

Placebo by Proxy

The placebo effect is so powerful, it has proven to even influence the behavior of a third party through an altered perception. This is known as the placebo-by-proxy effect. For instance, in one study, 58 children were demonstrating behavioral problems, so the parents brought them to therapy. The professional conducted some tests, and then informed the parents that the children were demonstrating a significant improvement in their behavior since the 'intervention' (at the time, the children had not). In follow up studies, not only did the parents report a reduction in the children's maladaptive behavior, the children actually demonstrated a tangible reduction in the problematic behaviors.[29] This raises the question: to what degree of culpability should educators be held liable for writing children off, or treating them as 'bad seeds'?

The Consensus of Reality

"For where two or three [or more] gather together in My name, there am I with them."

- Matthew 18:20

If an individual's reality can be altered through perception, intention, and expectation; what happens when two or more unite for a common cause? Several studies have assessed the impact of group meditation on local crime rates. In 1993, approximately 4,000 meditators gathered in Washington D.C. for about two months. The crime rates of the area were analyzed and compared with annual trends, weather, increased police force, population age changes, as well as the presence or increase of neighborhood watch programs. The study found a significant reduction (over 20%) in violent crime (homicides, rapes, and assaults), while the meditators gathered in DC.[30] A panel of experts across a spectrum of academia and governmental institutions participated in the research. The data indicates the results correlated strongly with the group size of the meditators. Meaning, more people meditating resulted in greater decreases in violent crime. Interestingly, robberies remained the same. Which may speak more so to the economic conditions of the area.

Much of how we gage and/or devote our lives, is based upon a consensus. For instance, athletes dedicate their lives to mastering a sport someone else created and decreed a game worth playing. When the sun is located at a specific point on the horizon in our solar system, it is said to represent a certain 'time' (of day, month, or year). Extrinsic factors influence the creation of systems to which many acquiesce. Our entire Life Force Energy can be spent engaging with these systems in one form or fashion. *Who are these Joneses that keep such an exhausting pace?* This need not be 'bad', but an awareness of its influence upon our choices, and therefore our lives, is necessary to make sure we are in tune with our Self and running our own race.

Seek and we shall find. I cannot tell you what reality to choose, but I can tell you this; we do choose our reality. The heart is the reel (real), the mind is the projector, 'reality' is the screen (veil). Awareness is choosing what we watch.

PEACE IS OUR CONNECTION TO THE ONENESS

The Path of Peace

🎼 *"Thinking Life and living Life are two very different things. The first one is harder than the last."*

- Goldfinger, "The Last Time"[31]

Through Peace, the path becomes clear, stabilizing our step. Ultimately, nothing can disturb our Peace, unless we choose to allow it to do so. There are some things we cannot change. To accept things as they are, does not mean to acquiesce to injustice, or put ourselves in harm's way. The crimes against humanity through the violence of slavery and war are beyond reconciliation. Even whispers echo. To engage with such a mindset in the hopes of changing it, will create lifetimes of frustration and despair. Powerful and humbling, we can only answer for our Self in this very moment. Peace escapes those who have yet to accept IT within themselves.

Realizing our ever-present Peace begins by asking "who is disturbed?" Becoming Aware of the space between thoughts, we find these disturbances to originate in the mind. *Then we must destroy the mind. Get it!* That's only going to create problems. Say our mind were some horrid creature out of a Stephen King novel. We've reached the climax of the movie. No longer willing to run from the torment of the mind,

39

we choose to stand and fight. Best yet, we're kicking the crap outta that wretched beast. Regardless of what's going on in the fight, we're still fighting! Therefore, we are engaged with the Energy of fighting. That is the frequency we are tuning to (remember the chapter on **focus**?). We have handed our Peace over to some fictional character. *Such is the mind.*

When we are not at Peace, it is through distraction, attachment, or engagement with internal or external stimuli. It's a labyrinth. However, all of this, regardless of how deep the wound, is still occurring on the surface of our being. As the saying goes, an inch of separation and the difference between Heaven and hell are known. At our core, we are Peace. We can tap into this Peace by emptying our mind and understanding the impermanence of the moment. The experience of Emptiness (Peace) will bring with it a great Compassion and realization of Oneness with all Existence.[32] This will be explored in greater detail throughout the remainder of this book and its Appendix.

How Do We Find the Moment?

"What if there isn't no tomorrow? There wasn't one today."

- Bill Murray, Groundhog Day

A movie is nothing more than the organization of still frame pictures. The illusion of sequence occurs once movement has been given to it. It's then embellished through sound and Light. Could the same not be said for Life? First there was sound. Then there was Light. The Voice then proclaimed…"Action!"

Every moment is new. Osho and Alan Watts have compared the moment to a river, a constant stream of now moments. When we attempt to grasp onto a moment too tightly, we miss it. It is like trying to carry a wave from the ocean. We may grab a handful of water, but the Energy behind it, that which made it a wave, will be lost to the tides. To Witness Life, is to allow it to flow unimpeded. It is our illusion of separateness that damns its river. Binding us to the insecurities of tomorrow, or the confines of yesterday. This very now moment is beyond all time and space. Mikhail Naimy has compared space to a Womb, and time its encasing.[33] As we shift and evolve our Consciousness, we are continuously birthed into new Wombs of the Universe. Every moment is a rebirth.

When 'finding' the moment, I like to give the example of the butterfly. Imagine, a butterfly with colors so bright our eyes widen as it flutters just in front of our face. Entranced, we think, "what a

41

beautiful butterfly." We've missed it! The moment cannot be categorized. To be present with the butterfly, is to move with the butterfly. To know and feel the flap of its wings as our own. What is 'beautiful' anyways? It is just a word layered with associations. We were not born knowing the word 'beautiful', or 'butterfly', or even 'I' for that matter.

Questions from My Friend:

In writing this book, I asked a Friend to read through the topics, and write down any questions she may have. I believe many of us have asked ourselves these same questions. These are included intermittently throughout the remaining chapters:

Why are we so intent on reliving the past, and not living in the moment?

People often live in the past because it is familiar. The now is new. Unchained and unharbored. We are vulnerable in the moment. The past has already occurred. We dealt with it as best we could. The past is nothing more than a previous now moment. The moments we were present, are those most cherished. Often recalled through the nostalgia of "better dayz". The future has yet to come, so we can distract ourselves with 'planning'. Conjuring a false sense of security. Like John Lennon said, "Life is what happens to you, while you're busy making other plans."[34] A moment of presence, and the past and future lose all relevance.

Are there too many technological distractions for human connections?

We are as distracted as we allow ourselves to be. Technology, like money, is neither good nor bad. It is the heart and intention of the user that determines its expression into this world. A device that fits into the palm of our hand, has connected our planet at the touch of a button. There is more technology inside our current smartphones, than was used to launch the first space shuttle![35] As much as technology may bridge distance, enlighten ignorance, and unite language, it has also served to blind us. Distraction is not interaction. Pokes and waves are a far cry from breaking bread with one another. At the mere threat of communion, people often flee for their phones as if a herd of stampeding elephants were trampling towards them. Buried head a source of solace.

Ironically, it is with technology that individuals are finding their way back to the present moment. There are over 1,300 phone apps dedicated to the practice of mindfulness. Individuals have reported a greater ability to cope with stressful events, as well as an improved sense of well-being and Life meaning as a result of using these apps.[36]

How do you practice being present - aside from putting down the devices or shutting off the TV?

The moment we are rushing towards, is no more important than the one we are in right now. When sitting, running, walking, talking, making Love, anything; drop the illusion of control. To Surrender to the present moment, is a death of sorts. Although false, it appears very real on its surface. It is this illusion of separation that placates hierarchies, perpetuates suffering, and emphasizes 'individuality' through persona (mask). The moment is GOD. As mentioned, the greatest vanity of the ego is to think it has the Power to separate from GOD.[37]

Peace sounds boring. Why would I want that?

Every moment is Divine. Flowing with Life, it is impossible to be bored. First off, who is there to be bored? Boredom is defined as a feeling of weariness due to a lack of interest or involvement in one's current activities.[38] So where does boredom originate? Boredom occurs by operating from the mind. Osho has declared boredom to be the result of intelligence. However, the expression, "bored out of our mind" could not be further from the Truth. For it is only the mind which is bored. When truly present, boredom cannot exist. Do flowers tire of their fragrance, or salmon become restless in their sojourn upstream? Does the sun long for retirement, or the ocean begrudge its tides?

If we found out that we had 12 hours to live, would we be bored? Probably not, right? How about 12 days? Still feels a little too close for comfort. We may prioritize spending this time with Family and Friends. Creating, sharing, and leaving a part of our Self for the world to enjoy in our absence. How about 12 weeks or twelve months? Would we still approach our daily activities with such zest for Life?

Boredom can be traced to the illusion that we will have this body, on this plane, for infinity. There are moments when we are awoken and shaken from this delusion. This is often spurred by loss. Natural 'disasters' have a way of quickly reminding us of our significant insignificance in the Cosmic order. As it has been given, so it can be taken without a moment's notice. We awaken, toss, turn, and then grumble back to sleep. Forgetting our brief reminder of how precious this Life really is.

Knowing that our time on this plane and in these bodies is limited, inspires action and Appreciation. We are Infinite in our potential. Through the practice of Self Love and Self-mastery, one loses the time to be bored. Partaking in just a couple of healthy activities each day, will keep one busy for lifetimes. The possibilities are endless. For example, this can include: meditation, stretching, yoga, exercising, cooking, healthy eating, time in nature, pleasure, laughter, reading, learning, exploring, creating, quality time with our Self, Family, or Friends.

The Guidance of Synchronicity

Pray for understanding, and let knowing blossom…

G OD, all that ever is, was and ever will be, is always speaking to us. Whether or not we listen, is up to us. GOD often begins by whispering. Offering hints and nudges. This may show up as a saying on a t-shirt, message on a billboard, or a slogan on a bumper sticker. Paying attention, we may hear the answer to a troublesome question in a nearby conversation, or in a song playing over a loudspeaker when we walk into a department store. All signs serve as a compass guiding us back home. Eventually, if enough time passes without listening (interesting ignorance is rooted in ignoring), we may get a Love tap on the back of the head. *Hey! Let's pull it together and get moving.* Next, maybe a shove on the shoulder. Sooner or later, if we continue to ignore GOD in our lives, we will be bitch slapped down to the ground, and reminded that ultimately, we don't run shit. As Romans 14:11 says, "every knee shall bow and tongue confess, that Lord is Lord."

Life Insurance

In the winter of 2014, a year after that difficult breakup mentioned in the introduction, I was back home visiting my Family for the holidays. While driving into the city, I was asking my Self if I should give it one more try. At that moment, I was guided to look up at a billboard on the southside of I-90. It was from an insurance carrier and read, "it's time to change Life partners." I couldn't make this up if I tried. I had my answer. The choice was up to me moving forward.

Know Thy Self

Growing up, we've been told a lot that does not apply to us. In fact, it's a flat out lie and contradiction to who we know we are. We are not subordinates. We are not helpless. We are not violent or untrustworthy. We are extensions and expressions of GOD in this physical plane.

The Universe is our university, experience its tenured professor. In order to learn, one must also be willing to forget. Unlike public schools, there is no shuffling through the system. We're not allowed to move on to the next course, until we complete this lesson plan. After we pass, we're then certified to share with others, so that we may help them along on their journey. The Life of a teacher is always that of a student, and vice versa.

Dr. Huey P. Newton is quoted as having said, "the best education is observation".[39] This is a vital skill, and discernment is key. Seeking Guidance and Wisdom from solely outside of our Self, can create chaos and mental instability. Ultimately, we are not separate from the Universe. However, we must be in alignment to receive its contributions. Our heart and gut are in constant contact with GOD. Peace is the bandwidth upon which we communicate. We're either present or we're not. It's really that simple. If we're present, our Life will reflect this by the amazing things that keep showing up to be Grateful for. The Universe echoes, what the heart has already spoken.

What is the Lesson I am Supposed to Learn Here?

B y recognizing patterns and cycles in our Life, we are better equipped to prevent their reoccurrence. Obviously, we don't touch a hot stove twice, but what about when the message is more subtle? During times of strife and struggle, it is often beneficial to ask our Self, "What is the lesson I am supposed to learn here?" Practicing this will help us to identify patterns and triggers in Life. Blind, deaf, and dumb; we will continue to experience the same negative feelings until the lessons are lEarned. These may take many a face and form, but the theme will remain the same. From my experience, romantic encounters are often the most telling of our needed lessons.

Find that which disturbs our Peace, and there we shall uncover our lesson. A difficult situation in Life can often be one of the best or worst things that has ever happened. I have heard on many occasion, Life does not happen to us, it happens for us. Broken bones, getting sick, loss of a job, et cetera can be viewed as an opportunity to slow down. To Appreciate more of what we have in this moment. It is our choice how we perceive it. All top performers, across all dynamics of human function (athletics, art, industry) have a special gift; they choose to see obstacles as opportunities.[40] In other words, they practice optimism and find the positive in all of Life's events.

Life has taught me to remain present during moments of pain. There is a direct correlation between Surrender and Witnessing. It is still happening, but it is not affecting the core of who I Am. This is not masochistic by any means. Though my early years may've warranted such decree. This is a technique that allows us to realize the Peace that exists within us, Infinitely and without condition. It's a lesson in nonattachment. Some moments present greater challenges. That's for certain. However, God does not give us that which we cannot handle. These lessons serve as a Guiding Light. A push back onto the right path. A reminder to breathe, be present, and Appreciate Life for what it is right now.

Why is it so Hard Getting Started?

For some reason, with anything that's good for us, the hardest part is often just getting started. This goes for anything. Changing our nutrition habits, exercising, removing negativity from our environment, stepping out of our comfort zone, or even meditating. When it comes to altering our current Life trajectory, starting over can be intimidating. The uncertainty of writing a new chapter can lead to paralysis. Postponing the new for the familiar. We find ourselves justifying unhappiness, and pacifying angst, remaining in relationships or careers that no longer serve us. However, as my Sister recently told me, we're not starting over from scratch. We're bringing all of our experience and Life lessons into this new moment.

If an elephant is chained from the time it is young, it will never attempt to escape. Even once its shackle has been removed. For it now believes wholeheartedly in its impressed upon limits. Starting over requires a leap of Faith, and Courage to face the unknown. However, think of the alternative?! Stay put and slowly piss our lives away. As we begin anew, our Life is rejuvenated with a sense of wonder and adventure. Our breath is fresh and our step is light. We are Free to create the Life of our dreams. Momentum builds discipline and strengthens commitment. We may stumble or skip a beat, however, interruption is never cessation. Every moment's a new opportunity. It only takes one snowflake to spawn an avalanche.

Understanding how our perception has been hijacked and shackled since our youth, how do we shake free of our chains? How do we remember that we are Free, Infinite beings? Divine expressions and extensions of GOD, imbibed with the Power to Co-Create. We remember, by forgetting. In doing so, our Peace is revealed.

DAILY IMPEDIMENTS TO PEACE

As we begin centering in our Peace, it's often shocking to Witness how busy our mind really is. This commotion appears amplified, only because it is in dramatic contrast to our original Silence. At this stage of development, many unnecessary problems can surface without a proper understanding into the workings of the mind. However, we needn't fight nor fret. A moment of Silence, and we have Awoken. Upon Awakening, that which is of no real value, is shaken from our Life like water from a dog's fur.

On the surface, this can appear in complete contradiction to what we thought our Life was 'supposed' to be. It may have looked like we were on the road to riches, stepping into that perfect relationship, or in a position to finally land that cake job. Although comfortable, this wouldn't have been fulfilling. There are few experiences more torturous, than knowing we are not living to our fullest potential. This section is designed to help us recognize common impediments to living in the moment and functioning from a state of Peace. A necessary ingredient when creating the Life of our dreams.

IDENTIFICATIONS

The Influence of Thoughts and Emotions

"Those who think they can, and those who think they can't, are both right."

- Confucius[41]

Know that from which thoughts arise.

Feel that from which thoughts arise.

Be that from which thoughts arise.

Pure Creative Conscious Energy.

When we speak, we are using breath. The same is true for while we are thinking, just as a subtler expression. Thoughts are electrical impulses (Energy), stimulating various regions of our emotional body.[42] That is why the content of our thoughts may trigger immense pleasure or tremendous pain. Further, the content of our thoughts (positive, self, others, past-related) has been associated with activating different cortical regions and state functions of the brain.[43] Thoughts such as judgment, anger, melancholy, expectations, and so on; blind us to the Peace existing within us right now.

Emotions are thoughts that have registered in the physical body. We can guide our emotions by choosing positive or negative thoughts. For example, the **perception** of danger will elicit an increase in the production of adrenaline in the kidneys. Whereas, arousal and pleasure releases serotonin in the spinal cord.

It's important to realize that the same event may be interpreted differently, depending on our past experiences and expectations. Jumping out of a plane, a negative remark from a stranger, or the cry of a baby all may trigger different thoughts, and therefore emotions, in various individuals. The jumpmaster may feel excitement, a monk may offer Compassion, or the Mother may seek to nurture.

Thoughts serve to form the structure of who we believe ourselves to be. They are carefully placed bricks, fortifying an identity. We like to think, this is a good thought or feeling, that's me. Those other ones are not. These thoughts about 'who we are' originate from a plethora of sources. These include, but are not limited to: family, friends, peers, teachers, neighbors, media, religious institutions, culture, and so on. When information (internally or externally) is presented in opposition to what we think about ourselves, a great turmoil (more thoughts) blows in like a storm in the open sea. We feel vulnerable.

Anything we label as ourselves, is only a thought. Whatever word we have learned/been taught and now hinged our identity upon, is nothing more than a thought. Regardless of who or how many cosign to its authenticity. Choosing various thoughts (ideologies) to represent us only leads to difficulty. It creates a split. Not only amongst 'others', but within ourselves. Comparison prevents connection.

Thoughts are either of the past or the future. No thought can truly exist in the present moment. It's impossible. However, we cannot forcefully stop our thinking. For who is the one putting an end to these thoughts? The mind is only fighting with itself, subtly judging the very thoughts rendered.

Questions:

1. Who have I believed myself to be up until now? Who do I want to be?

   _____

   _____

   _____

2. Who/what have I been told that I am (start at the beginning)?

   _____

   _____

   _____

> **Anything we label as ourselves, is only a thought.**

How to Stop Negative Thinking?

Osho has presented a helpful conceptualization of the mind. He suggests that, to even refer to it as a mind is inaccurate, because this creates the impression that it is an object. Mind is an activity, and it would be more accurate to describe it as 'minding'.[44] Similar to walking. Walking cannot be left anywhere. When it's done, it's done. Same with minding. It is a process. So often we have been conditioned to believe that the mind is this elusive separate being. Hiding in the crevices of our unconscious, bent on defeating our well-intentioned transcendence. I know I battled with this in meditation for years. *I'm gonna find you, and you're gonna get it!* Minding in action.

We stop negative thinking by Witnessing the space from which thoughts arise (the meditation practices explored in the Appendix provide tools for honing this skill). First this will appear as quick gaps in thought. A momentary space of Silence between the constant chatter. Through daily practice, the gaps expand. We are no longer the servant of a mind run wild. To touch Silence, is to know Peace.

Why do Good People do Bad Things?

W hen trying to comprehend the atrocities of this world, it is important to understand why a person is knowingly willing to engage in such acts. For example, participating in the genocide of Native Americans, the concentration camps of nazis, the killing fields of Cambodia, or the dropping of two nuclear bombs on entire cities of children, women, and men in Japan. In the early 1960's, researcher Stanley Milgram conducted an experiment to answer these very questions. His findings shook the scientific community, and left our beliefs about human nature shattered.[45]

In the study, participants were given the impression that they were assigned to one of two roles. Either that of teacher or student. They were informed that the study would be assessing an individual's ability to expedite learning. This would be accomplished by pairing errors in memory, with the negative consequence of an electric shock. The voltage would be purposively intensified with every incorrect answer.

After meeting and drawing straws, the participants were separated into teacher and student. The 'teacher' was always the participant, and the 'student' was always the confederate (a third party secretly involved in the experiment). The participant was escorted to a room to witness the confederate being strapped to a chair and hooked up to a device. The participant remained in an adjacent room, accompanied by an authoritative figure in a grey lab coat. The room contained a transmitter believed to administer varying degrees of electricity to the student.

The confederate's responses were prerecorded to provide consistency throughout the experiment. The participants were informed that the 'student' had a heart condition. They were aware that a particular level of voltage could potentially kill this individual. The confederate was perceived to be just another random participant who drew the short end of the straw. Both having equal opportunity to be in this position. Therefore, it was understood that the student was innocent and of no wrong doing, other than incorrectly answering the questions.

During the experiment, the student begged for help, eventually demanding to be unstrapped and released at once. The authoritative figure directed the participants to continue. The participants expressed concern and reluctance to do so. They were again ordered to proceed. When it looked as if the participants were unwilling to continue, they were given one of the following four prompts: (1) please continue; (2) the experiment requires you to continue; (3) it is absolutely essential that you continue; or (4) **you have no other choice but to continue**.

Most astonishing, 65% of participants continued to the highest level of voltage (450 volts). All participants distributed a shock of up to 300 volts. Milgram's study demonstrated that people are willing to participate in a behavior that may kill an innocent person, if told to do so by someone perceived as an 'authority'. This does not mean the individual did so gleefully. The participants were often distraught and in deep moral conflict while engaging in the behavior. The authoritative figure ensured the participants they were absolved of responsibility, as they were acting appropriately under his orders. Again, 65% of the participants were willing to induce the maximum voltage of electricity to a fellow human being begging for his Life. Knowing one flick of the switch may cause death.

So what influenced the participants to take matters so far? One, the man in the lab coat was presented, and therefore perceived, as a designated authority in the environment. When and where else have we acquiesced our Power to those who claim to know better than us? Did the grey lab coat serve that much of an influence in directing human behavior?

A Mind Incarcerated

Philip G. Zimbardo's 1971 Stanford prison experiment examined this very question.[46] A group of young men were randomly selected to serve as either a prisoner, or guard. The guards and inmates were both garbed in a wardrobe suited for their role. Participants selected as prisoners, were arrested at their home and brought to Stanford University. A prison was replicated in the basement of the psychology building. By day six, the two-week experiment was shut down. The 'guards' were physically and mentally harming the 'prisoners', while the 'prisoners' were becoming depressed and severely stressed. A riot occurred in which the prisoners revolted against the guards. The prisoners going so far as barricading themselves in their cells, and setting fire to a mattress.

Milgram's research assessed an individual's willingness to submit to an authoritative figure, even when behaving in direct contradiction to one's moral code. Zimbardo's Stanford prison experiment illuminated the dangers of group norms through role identification. Both studies serve a grave reminder to the Power of perception. Costumes dictate roles. Roles direct personality.

The Compilation of Ego

🎼 *"Who made up words? Who made up numbers? And what kind of spell is mankind under?"*[47]

- Nas in his collab with Damian Marley, on their song "Patience"

The mind has been conditioned to interpret 'reality' through a limited five senses (sight, smell, hearing, taste, and touch). It is then indoctrinated to perceive the world (and ourselves) through limits, potential, or 'defining' characteristics. For example, Dr. Gibson's book, "Race: The Root of all Evil", illuminates how the concept of 'race' is false and utilized for conquest.[48] Justifying divisiveness and bigotry through illusion. Even how we perceive color is completely backwards to how this actually occurs.

An object will appear a certain color by reflecting that color and absorbing the other colors in the spectrum. For example, a blue balloon only appears blue because it is reflecting blue and absorbing all other colors of Light touching its surface. Further, the range of human sight only sees a fraction of the 'known' Light spectrum. And this is just one frequency existing in space and time.

Time has been described as change.[49] In the movie "Lucy", Scarlett Johansen's character defined time as the "measurement of movement". Time also serves to form identity. How can we be of any real age, when time is a manmade construct? Our biological age even varies from our chronological age. Ever meet someone who looked and acted young for their age? Yes, 'years' are measured by laps around the sun, because that is what we have accepted. However, there are approximately forty calendars simultaneously keeping track of 'days' at this very moment.[50] The Chinese calendar has thirteen months during a leap year based on solar and moon cycles, and it wasn't until 1949 that it was ordered to be in accord with the Gregorian calendar.[51] So, who's is 'correct'? That may depend on the geography of one's birth.

A Play on Words

"The more words we know, the more things we can see."

- KRS One, "Just Like That"[52]

We have been conditioned to navigate our internal and external world through our words. Remember the power of labels? These words then serve to conceptualize our reality into a fixed understanding. Although words often limit our interactions, they can also open our eyes to a whole new world. For instance, understandings into Energy Bodywork such as Reiki, Tai Chi, and Qi Gong can heal the sick. Knowing the principles of Tantra and the Tao one can experience thousands of orgasms, simply by remaining present and breathing while making Love. One navigates the dream world, by understanding techniques to induce lucid dreaming. The knowledge of a wave particle in quantum physics, moves one from a linear individual, to the realization of an Infinite being functioning in a multidimensional Universe. Where past, present and future occur simultaneously.

The Power of Words

"Words, at best, are but an Honest lie".

- Mikhail Naimy, in the "Book of Mirdad"[53]

Speak, and we will manifest. However, pay attention to the script. What story are we narrating? If we have a 'bad' day, do we repeat it to 'others', hoping for them to 'affirm' it? Instead of listening to the words, feel the words. Go deeper. Feel their sound. Be present with their vibration through our bodies. Language has a tendency to intellectualize Life, forgetting that worth communicating is beyond words.

Creating a New Story

1. Be mindful of our internal dialogue. What words do we use when times get tuff, or we find ourselves in conflict?

2. How we feel at that moment, will indicate the effect of those words upon our Spirit.

3. Be aware of why and when we say "I can't" to something.

    - Is it a choice, or are we excusing this "can't" to something out of our control?

4. Find a list of words we can substitute that are positive and affirming.

    - Even, "I do not want to do that" is more positive and assertive than "I can't". Bringing with it a rejuvenated sense of control over our lives.

5. Write these affirming words down and practice saying them out loud a couple of times until they feel natural.

6. Be mindful of the labels we attach to people, places, things, and most importantly, our Self.

7. As discussed previously, use symbols to our advantage. Create new, positive and inspiring associations with external stimuli that remind us to breathe, be at Peace, and vibrate from a place of Appreciation. Doing so, our Life will hum along.

8. We are the authors to our book. Choose words that will convey a story we would enjoy reading. All we have to do now is Live it! As Joe Rogan and Kevin Hart explained, even if it sucked up until now, that was just the first chapter. Every hero starts with a past. It's what we do beginning right now that counts.

LETTING GO OF EXPECTATIONS

Judgment is an Expectation

"Judge not, lest Ye be judged."

- Matthew 7:1

What's so 'wrong' about being wrong? What's so 'right' about being right? It's a desperate attempt to solidify an ego as existing superior to another human being. A superfluous hierarchy, ignorant of our Eternal connection. Now all that's needed is to determine where on the social/moral ladder we reside. *What a vista! If I step on that other guy's head, I might be able to see my house from here!*

Oftentimes, our judgments of 'others' are really just projections of an unsettled feeling within our Self. When we judge, or are angry, we are the ones left carrying the burden. The judged, or the target of our anger, does not bear this load. It is us who choose to lug it into the next moment. Anger results from someone failing to meet our expectations. These are often hinged upon some future desired outcome. Confronted with the fear that we are not in complete control of everything in our universe, we judge the degenerate. It's delusional. How is an extension of GOD, not worthy of GOD?

Judging our Failures

"Failure gave me strength. Pain was my motivation."

- Michael Jordan[54]

How willing are we to surrender the illusion that we know better than GOD. As mentioned in the chapter on Peace, often the worst things in our lives, offer the opportunity to be some of the best. It just depends on our perspective and time frame with which we view these events. Would anyone give a damn about that tower in Pisa, had it not survived an unstable foundation and the merits of its doubters? On Tim Ferriss' podcast, two young entrepreneurs, who built an eight figure Amazon business, suggest that it is more beneficial to perceive 'failures' as feedback.[55] An opportunity to improve upon previous design.

We may judge a failure as the worst experience of our Life, but when we reflect three years from now, a year from today, in a month; who knows?! It's hard to imagine how sorry we'd be, had we continued on that trajectory. As my friend Nuriel once revealed, "at the worst of our worst, the lowest of our lows, we still have LOVE." When I hit that low, I burst into laughter. I finally felt that LOVE. It had been with me the entire time. Ever walk around the house looking for your keys, only to find you were carrying them around?

When Does Discernment Become Judgment?

The moment "I" enters the picture. As has been mentioned, we often identify ourselves by our beliefs. When these come into question or under scrutiny, ego swoops to the rescue. Anger brandishes a butter knife like its wielding the Excalibur. We fight, not because we're defending a 'belief', but rather, an identity we have formed for ourselves around that belief. Even when presented with evidence to the contrary. If we do not feel validated, it is because we are still seeking validation. In the midst of discord, we become deaf, dumb, and blind to Love. Walking away, conflict fades into the distance. When we go within, it never existed to begin with.

A Practice...

What would happen if we didn't judge for a day? Even just a morning or afternoon? Let's say an hour. Make this a meditation. Set the alarm and watch. Remember, even if we find ourselves judging, don't judge our Self for doing so. Just recognize, give thanks, and correct by breathing into our Peace/Silence.

> **If we do not feel validated, it is because we are still seeking validation.**

I Desire to be Desireless

Desires compartmentalize the human being. They prevent us from living fully in the moment. Waiting for tomorrow to enjoy today. Achieve these desires, and new desires are born. Desire is an abyss pulling at restless minds. There is nothing wrong with vision. However, it's difficult to cross a mountainous terrain focused solely on the horizon. Looking too far ahead, we may miss a step and drown in a stream, when we could have swam and coasted through the valley.

Truth cannot be realized and shared through the vanity of tomorrow, or the saga of yesterday. When we are present, we can only trust. Truth shines in the very here and now. It is our judgments and desires that cast shadows upon its Light. Desire is a subtle Energy of the mind that can be felt when we are present. Desires come in all sorts of shapes and sizes. Material or spiritual gain, physical pleasure, recognition, letting go, achievement, et cetera. Desires often justify usury and manipulation. Treating people as a means to an illusory ends. At the end of the day, desires are merely thoughts that take us out of the present moment, disconnecting us from our Peace.

Giving Freely

We have been misled to believe that others will follow suit and treat us as we treat them. This holds a particular beauty, however effaces the Joy and Freedom of Life. Nobody owes us a damn thing. Expectations shackle both the giver and benefactor. Only an open hand has something to offer.

Helping for the sake of helping is beautiful. However, even that may bear a bit of selfishness when we go deep within. If it did not feel good, would we still do so? If pain resulted, does this feed any self-serving martyr complex? Does it serve to subtly separate the 'helped' from the 'helper'? Maybe, maybe not. Only we know. True helping occurs in the moment. Most else is often a bargain for recompense. Meaning, some future pay off or reconciling of a past debt.

How benevolent is it to offer assistance to anyone (family, friend, or 'stranger'), under the condition they sign a promissory note in blood to be at our beck and call? Being mindful of our intentions, research indicates that giving support to others provides us with a litany of Health benefits. These include, but are not limited to: improved mental health, increased feelings of well-being, reduced depressive symptoms, lowered blood pressure and heart rate, as well as a decreased risk of mortality.[56]

Often, we are taught to help beyond our means. To sacrifice for the betterment of another. The concept of utilitarianism, when mindful of human rights, has a certain nobleness to it. However, an empty hand will eventually need to seek its own nourishment. Hungry and reduced to scavenging. Beyond food and external resources, this is especially true of our Peace. Bear in mind, this is by no means a proclamation to horde. Only a reminder to be mindful of ulterior motives.

Giving takes many forms. This can mean our time, attention, and/or material support. We need not be millionaires to help those in need. Simply by paying attention, a person will feel Respected and understood. When we give without expectation, we not only release the beneficiary of any alleged obligation, but we Free our Self from the burden of 'keeping score'. As is said, "Live light. Travel Light. Be the Light. Share the Light." The sun shines for that is its nature. It seeks not praise, approval, or celebration. It is rewarded in its very being. Presence is the gift that keeps on giving.

> Expectations shackle both the giver and benefactor. Only an open hand has something to offer.

Where the Hell is This?

"What is normal for the spider, is chaos for the fly."

- Charles Addams[57]

It's been said that the path to hell is paved with good intentions. During my days at the charity, I'd need a tetanus shot after hearing this. I'd go rabid. At that time, I believed this was just an excuse to not 'do good'. To justify manipulation, and pacify feelings of guilt over selfishness. Really, the *intention* of that person's statement, was often to inform me that a Loving heart does not make up for poor business planning. For example, giving away all of our money to *help* people in need, while day to day, month to month, we struggled financially. To say we were a charity, sums it up pretty well.

Intentions and expectations can often be confused. For example, let's say my intention is to share and spread Love throughout my Life. Waiting in rush hour traffic, I decide to let someone cut in front of me. Perfect, I've made someone's Life a little easier. Now let's say, that person darts out in front of me and doesn't provide a wave, smile, or nod of Appreciation. Maybe they do. Perhaps they mean mug and flick me off. Maybe they smug with entitlement as they slowly creep out in front of me. What is my response? Was it really my intention to share and spread Love wherever I go? Or, was I seeking recognition?

It is irrelevant how the 'other' person behaves in response to my gesture. Too often we chalk it up to, "they're just a bad person" or "they're evil." Really? Because they didn't acknowledge our benevolence and uncanny ability to hold our right foot on the brake pedal five seconds longer than the preceding car? Ultimately, we never know what is transpiring in someone else's Life. Especially when operating from the head. If we did, we'd treat each other with much greater Compassion. It's not our job to figure out the intentions of another. The heart knows. Allow that to be the guiding force.

Let Love resound in our breath, not be camouflaged or decorated in our words. If our intention is to spread Love, this is just another opportunity to do so. Fruition begins well before the seed is planted. Nothing someone does will change our intention. It will only reveal it.

> Let Love resound in our breath, not be camouflaged or decorated in our words.

ALONENESS VS. LONELINESS

"Because you don't know your aloneness, there is fear and you feel lonely, so you want to cling to something."

- Osho[58]

L oneliness will convince a person to stay in a relationship when the gut says leave. It is a beggar and masochist, constantly seeking attention. Loneliness pointedly engages in distraction and busy work. Nothing is ever really accomplished, but much is lost. Aloneness can only know Love. Loneliness nitpicks and bickers. Aloneness knows one's value, and is unwilling to accept anything less. Aloneness is comfortable doing nothing, centered in Witnessing. Secure and at home in Silence.

On the path of Awakening, we may feel loneliness at times. Seeking answers, validation, and comradery outside of our Self. This is perfectly normal. We only need recognize its occurrence. This is how Witnessing our thoughts, emotions, and behaviors moment to moment can guide us back to our Higher Self. The heart is a compass, Peace its true north. The further the distance, the greater the disturbance. Lost abroad, anger turns to rage, nervousness escalates to stress, and sadness slumbers to depression. If we find ourselves lost in the web of loneliness, remember, it can only occur in the mind, through thought. Aloneness exists in the present moment, as the moment. Never really alone...

Another Question from My Friend:

Why does loneliness correlate with an empty feeling? Why are people afraid to be alone?

Oftentimes, people are afraid to be alone, because they are fearful of being with themselves. When alone, there is no one to blame for their uncomfortable feelings. People seek refuge in others. This is why numerous scientific studies have demonstrated that addictive behaviors are significantly reduced through social support systems [once an individual's basic needs (food, clothing, and shelter) are met].

Loneliness correlates with an empty feeling because we have yet to find ourselves. A feeling of 'emptiness' (not to be confused with 'Emptiness') is a searching for someone or something to momentarily fill the void. Once we find our Self, it is impossible to ever be lonely or bored. This is why so many relationships lack foundation. People haven't studied themselves, and want someone else to teach them. They seek identification through the partnership. The person was discontent, and sought Peace externally.

> **Once we find our Self, it is impossible to ever be lonely or bored.**

Escapism

The world as presented through mainstream media and the public education system, can cause people to lose their shit. Combine this with a distressed, unstable household, and children are walking timebombs. As they enter adulthood, every effort has been made to convince them of scarcity. That the real treasure lies outside today, and is hinged upon another's approval. Those who see themselves and this world differently, are often ridiculed then ostracized.

Ostracization has detrimental consequences on the victim. Undermining the person's sense of control, belonging, self-esteem, meaningfulness, willingness to participate in pro-social behavior, and even increases aggression.[59] We are social beings by nature. In ancient times, exile was equated with a death sentence.[60] Feeling we do not belong to a group (family, friends, peers, social, economic, religious, etc.) can be dehumanizing and debilitating. When it becomes too much to bear, a person may seek escape by any means possible. A blaze of glory or an overdose, a rope and a suicide note.

Losing Loved ones to suicide is never easy. We not only mourn their loss, we often blame ourselves for their passing. For not reaching out one more time. Not being so empathetic and *really listening* to what they were *trying* to tell us. Sometimes the escape is not so final. Escape can often pass itself off as busyness, losing ourselves in thought patterns or maladaptive behaviors. In hopes of discovering a moment of solace, our search for refuge will scratch upon every nook and cranny of this Earth. Hence, the appeal of drugs and alcohol. They numb us to our feelings and excuse our behaviors. Offering us a glimpse of what it looks like to be Free and out of our head. If only for a moment.

Substances such as drugs and alcohol serve to engage the body's chemistry. Either to its benefit or detriment. As George Carlin reminds us:

> Drugs are wonderful when you try them for the first time. They're not around for millennia for no reason. And as you keep using, the pleasure part decreases, and the pain part, the price you pay, increases. Until the balance is completely the other way, and it's almost all pain, and there's hardly any pleasure. At that point, you would hope, that the intellect says, 'oh. Ooohh. This doesn't work anymore. I'm going to die if I don't do something.' But you need people around you that can help you, and you need something to live for. You have to have something to live for.[61]

Decades of research indicate that personality traits, fears, strengths, and Life experiences can be passed through the DNA.[62] Addiction is no different, however, it is a choice. Ultimately, anything can serve as an addiction. For example, when trying to quit smoking weed. We have made the decision to no longer toke. Then a stranger, acquaintance, or even an old friend offers us a hit. That is not the Universe saying, "go ahead, hit that blunt; you deserve it." As the decision to quit has already been made. This is the Universe asking, "do you really want this out of your Life, and if so, to what extent?"

We will know what to allow into our Life, by remaining present in our body. If it creates fear, doubt, or just a really bad feeling; it no longer has a place in our Life. Substituting old, maladaptive behaviors with new, healthy choices is powerful in lessening the crippling effects of addiction.[63] Understanding our motives will lend tremendous weight in letting go of our compulsions. Many of these wounds can be traced to childhood. Understanding what the behavior is doing to our body, is also helpful in finding reasons to quit. Though, this is often not enough when it comes to addiction, as Self Love has yet to be discovered. For this reason, meditation is a game changer. It is the most intimate relationship we will ever know. Research has demonstrated that mindfulness significantly reduces or eliminates addictive thought patterns and/or behaviors.[64] Touching the core of our being, we are pulled in the direction of our Life's purpose.

The Shadow of Paranoia

"The enemy has only images and illusions, behind which he hides his true motives. Destroy the image, and you will break the enemy."

- Bruce Lee's Teacher in "Enter the Dragon"[65]

There is an old African proverb that guides, "when there is no enemy within, the enemy outside can do us no harm".[66] Although any concept of an external world is ultimately an illusion, while walking the path of illumination, shadows may appear. These are reflections of our internal being. Casings that need to be broken through. Illusions of "them", can serve as helpful guides. Providing inspiration to ask our Self the tuff questions. Where do I have hate? When am I violent? How do I express a lack of Trust? Am I jealous or insecure?

Ultimately, we are everything and nothing at the same time. Even darkness is of the Light. However, this does not mean we need to express those demons, or even take 'ownership'. For instance, some wounds may be ancestral. Showing up as negative thoughts or feelings when triggered. Regardless of the catalyst, acknowledge, accept, and allow this uneasiness to pass without continued attention or engagement. Breathe and Witness them for what they are: merely thoughts. This removes the tension and fear found at this stage of Awakening.

For me this was a difficult juncture, and often led to uncertainty and inaction. I would wonder, "why would I think that? How could I harbor such monstrosities? Oh my God, is this really who I am? Should I just throw myself off of the roof and save the world from this?" If you find your Self in this stage of Awakening right now, you will get through it. I promise. The butterfly sheds its cocoon and doesn't give a second thought to the caterpillar it left behind.

Them and Us

As our Consciousness expands, sensitivity is increased. Therefore, it becomes increasingly important to deliberately choose the frequency of our vibration. The paranoia of 'them' can destroy a psyche. Especially in a society that deliberately suppresses our Awakening. In the 'west', without the Love and support of a family or community, mediums and seers are labeled as schizophrenic.[67] Berated into paranoia and isolation. Outside of 'western' culture, these same 'seers' are regarded as Shamans and sought out for their Wisdom. The church appears threatened by these gifted mediums. Shamans have been tortured and murdered under religious inquisition for millennia. Institutions attempting to monopolize commune with GOD. *You wanna talk with God? Now you gotta go through me.*

So, what does a seer or medium really do? She or he is able to peer into a different spectrum of reality. As mentioned previously, everything in 'reality' occurs simultaneously. It has nothing to do with the physical eyes. The expansion of Consciousness is through vibration, allowing for greater access and mobility through dimensions.

The individual is able, through training or birthright, to perceive Life with a wider lens so to speak.

This is not as unusual as it may first appear. For instance, look at Life on this planet right now. Canines are able to hear well beyond the capabilities of most humans. Hence, the Power of dog whistles. Reindeer, another mammal, can perceive into the ultraviolet spectrum of Light. I am willing to bet that many people reading this, have gifts and abilities that were stifled "for our own good". Ensuring others wouldn't make fun of us for being crazy. As people across this planet continue to Awaken, those embracing these gifts will eventually be considered the norm. Our species is evolving, and our Consciousness expanding. The dark ages are over. We are entering the age of Illumination.

HEAVEN RIGHT NOW

HAPPY, HEALTHY, & STRONG

"We school our children in history, mathematics, and language, but not in happiness, strength, and health – the most important values of life itself!"

- Wim Hof, The Iceman[68]

The leading cause of death in the world is heart disease.[69] Interestingly, Love is what our planet needs most right now. The following is a chronological list of the top ten causes of death in the United States: heart disease, cancer, chronic lower respiratory disease, accidental (stumbling, traffic, legal and illegal overdose, etc.), stroke, alzheimer's, diabetes, influenza and pneumonia, kidney disease, and suicide.[70] Nearly seventy-five percent of all deaths in the U.S. are linked to the aforementioned.[71] Not violence, as the media would lead us to believe. The media hypes a fear of 'others', when in 'reality' we are our own greatest threat. Yet, when was the last time John Walsh warned viewers that 'laziness', a known killer, had escaped captivity and was running amuck? *I wonder how much I could get for a bounty? Eh, that's a lot of work, I'll check on it tomorrow.*

Much of these illnesses can be prevented, and sometimes even corrected, by a healthy lifestyle. As Wim Hof shares, this boils down to being happy, healthy, and strong.[72] Holistically, this involves a balance between mental, physical, emotional, sexual, social, and spiritual health. The following chapters explore these components in greater detail. As we move forward, I offer the guidance of Bruce Lee, "absorb what is useful, discard what is not, and add what is specifically your own."[73]

Life is a Meditation (22 Techniques in Appendix)

"Eighty percent of world class performers meditate."

- Tim Ferris[74]

A long the path of Life, every step is a prayer. Every breath an Awakening. We do not meditate to become 'Holier than thou'. Hit it for ten minutes in the morning, then leave it alone the rest of the day. We meditate to sharpen our sword. So that when we need to use it, we're ready. It's like fighting. The heavy bag doesn't hit back (usually). It affords us a space to master our jabs, crosses, hooks, and footwork. Then, when moving through this world, if these skills are needed for self-defense, we are prepared.

Once 'out there' (which is still just another Here), if a troublesome thought, emotion, or event occurs, we are present with it. Just as we were in meditation. A wave that would've dispersed a village, barely touches the shores in the still waters of our mind. One of the first methods to creating balance in our Life, is to remove our identification with our Self as the mind. It is like the wind identifying itself with the leaves with which it rustles. Ignorant to its omnipresence. Meditation is a tool to not only quiet the mind, but it lays the foundation to realize that we are not the mind! A simple glimpse into this Truth, and we are no longer its servant.

Research into Meditation

Researchers have attempted to equate the effects of meditation with psychological relaxation techniques.[75] However, a comparative meta-analysis indicates that meditation is significantly more effective in positively altering psychological variables.[76] These include, but are not limited to: cognition, learning, memory, intelligence, neuroticism, anxiety, stress, attention, perception, mindfulness, personality, empathy, emotional regulation, self-concept, well-being, and self-realization. Prolonged practice leads to an 'automated' regulation of behavior.[77] Meaning, we don't *try* to be at Peace when something disturbs us, we just are. Peace is our nature.

Meditation also improves focus, memory, emotional regulation, and neurological functioning.[78] As we are better equipped to cope with stress (and no longer identify with it), practicing mindfulness enhances our immune systems. [79] Practitioners further report experiencing greater self-compassion, body awareness, physical well-being, and Life satisfaction.[80]

Don't Forget to Breathe

As we learned in the previous section, thoughts are simply a subtle version of breath. Therefore, regaining control of our breath, is an excellent and easy way to quiet internal noise. Relatedly, research indicates breathing interventions improve emotional regulation.[81] Basically, how we breathe, equates to how we feel. Breathing is subject to both voluntary and nonvoluntary control by the practitioner through complex feedback mechanisms.[82] Breathing regulation provides an excellent means to immediately alter our physiology.[83]

Breathwork is powerful in interrupting the relationship between stimulus and conditioned response. For example, reducing PTSD symptoms in trauma survivors.[84] By remaining present with our breath, we become aware that we are not our thoughts, thereby breaking any identification with maladaptive thought patterns. The deeper we connect with our breath, the greater intimacy we will experience with our Self and our partners. Through breathing, our orgasmic nature is revealed.

Making Time

All of us have time to meditate in the morning. It is simply a matter of where we choose to direct our Energy. If we have time to scroll through social media, we have time to meditate. If we have time to watch television or YouTube, we have time to meditate. If we have time to bitch, whine, or gossip, trust me, there's time. The question is: what do we prioritize in our Life?

Even if we have to wake up early, usually there's something we can cut out at the back end to make up for it. It may suck the first couple of days, but the body will quickly adapt to the new practice, and our Life will be forever enhanced for it. It only takes a short distance to go a long ways. In 22 days, behaviors turn to habits.

Helpful Hint:

Setting an alarm while meditating allows us to forget about time and feel deeper into the moment. Sitting cross-legged on a cushion with the hands resting on top of one another is a common position that we can do anywhere. After a morning meditation, reading a quick page or two of a spiritually enhancing book will do wonders for the remainder of the day.

The Breadth of Meditation

Ultimately, anything can serve as a meditation. It is simply a tool used to remove egoic barriers, such as judgment or attachment, and melt into a state of Witnessing. Present and centered in Peace. When meditating, various blockages or buried sentiments may find their way to the surface. The preceding chapters were intended to provide a framework for Witnessing their occurrence, so as not to become disenchanted by their appearance.

The Appendix provides a variety of meditation techniques. Various personalities will be drawn to different methods, and that's ok. There's no right or wrong technique. Find what works best, or play around with several of them, **one at a time**. To preview, the techniques explore the following practices: breathing, Witnessing, listening, visualizing, and, but not limited to, sexual pleasure.

Accepting Right Now

We will never have another experience like this one right now. The sights, sounds, smells, feelings, and so on, are all unique to this moment. Recognize the clouds of the mind for what they are, fleeting and transient. No cloud has yet to leave a mark on the sky. Meditation reminds us that there is nothing to be done. We are perfect and perfecting RIGHT NOW. Ultimately, there is no becoming. Only being.

The Power of Movement Meditation

Meditative movement, is the practice of remaining present and focused while moving. Meditative movements, such as Tai Chi and Qi Gong, have demonstrated remarkable health benefits for young and old practitioners.[85] Qi Gong is discussed in greater detail in the Appendix. It is an ancient art, considered by many, to be related to Tai Chi, Kung Fu, and other forms of the martial arts.[86] Tibetan Shaolin monks are renowned for their incorporation of Qi Gong into their feats of Power, Strength, and endurance. This includes, but is not limited to, drying wet sheets on their heads while sitting naked in the snow, absorbing blows to the body from a sledge hammer, snapping a speared bamboo stick with their jugular, or taking an electric drill to the skull (don't try this at home).[87] Yoga is another movement meditation that can produce profound changes in one's body. Not only is it phenomenal for flexibility and Strength conditioning, but also rehabilitation.

Arthur Boorman

Arthur Boorman served as a paratrooper in the Gulf war and could no longer walk without the use of crutches.[88] He gained a lot of weight, and had nearly given up on Life. He knew Yoga was his answer to a better Life. After hundreds of instructors turned him down, he eventually he found someone willing to work with him. Repeatedly he fell on his face. More importantly however, every single time he fell, he picked himself up. "Just because I can't do it today, doesn't mean that I'm not gonna be able to do it someday." After six months of daily

Yoga, he had lost a hundred pounds, and was walking without crutches. Following a year of falling and picking himself up, Arthur's video ends with him sprinting full speed down the street.

Conscious Sex (Sexual Pleasure Meditations in Appendix)

"When sex becomes a meditation it flowers into Love, and this flowering is a movement towards the Divine."

- Osho[89]

My experience with sex and sexual Energy has been greatly influenced by the teachings of Osho, Shantam Nityama, Shophar Graves, Mantak Chia, Sasha Cobra, and Yao Morris. As Life is the best teacher, I further want to pay homage to my Partners who have shared their most intimate of Self with me. I am forever Grateful. Additionally, I would like to thank the clients I have served through the Energy Bodywork sessions. As always, we cannot heal without being healed, and cannot serve without being served. Knowing that all healings, blessings, and service are an expression and extension of GOD. Moving forward, the reader may substitute personal sexual preferences while exploring the ensuing content.

The Nature of Sex

Sexual Energy is Life Force Energy.[90] IT is the essence of our nature. Each of us is here right now because of sex. It is nothing to fear, condemn, or lust after. Yet in a society supposedly so free, curiosity and desire have been beaten into the fetal position. We have shackled ourselves to others' promiscuity. Caged in the promise that someone else knows best.

Sex is not about doing something to someone, or performing with a certain aptitude. So often we do something, to get somewhere. Usually, somewhere outside the moment. Holding hands to kiss, kissing to undress, naked to penetrate. Forgetting the bliss and intimacy of right now.

The greater our presence, the more we realize that 'we' really aren't doing anything. We are vessels for this LOVE to flow through. Melting into The Oneness. Not only are we kissing our partner's lips, we are making Love with their whole being. Therefore, rather than saying, "I Love you", let our touch be our words. Appreciation our mantra. Presence its annunciation.

At the heights of orgasm, that which is brought forth through thoughts, feelings, and sounds is superimposed with an Energy that births worlds. Plain and simple, do not fuck around with this. If not operating from our highest vibration, wait Patiently. Sex heals, but it is a mutual transmutation. Do not unleash one's woes on an unsuspecting partner. The daily cultivation of presence though Peace, Love, and Gratitude will serve to shed that which is no longer beneficial in our lives.

∞ *For greater insights and techniques to heal trauma and dive deeper into our bliss, please see the section on sexual pleasure meditations located in the Appendix.*

Understanding Men and Women

Both sexes contain various degrees of feminine and masculine Energy within. They are two expressions of the same Energy. Two sides to the same coin. The feminine Energy is passive and receptive (magnetic), while the masculine Energy engages and penetrates (electric).

It is a man's nature to have his Power reflected back to him through sex.[91] However, it should be to his partner's benefit. No man should ever be a beggar. Seeking to gain 'something'. It is our offering that is of significance. Therefore, Conscious connection requires a deep understanding of our intention prior to intimately relating (ultimately all relating is intimate). The male ego is often, yet unwittingly, seeking validation. Prioritizing conquest rather than enjoying exploration.

A woman is an availability.[92] Every Womb is special for IT brings forth Life. Each must be nourished, protected, and Loved. Her Universe cries for us to know the subtleties of who she is. To feel received in her Love, and safe in her giving. Her heart must run wild and Free, for this is her nature. Men do not 'grant' her any special 'permission' to do so. It is through Appreciation and a total acceptance of her authentic being.

Another Question from My Friend:

How do I meet someone I want to be with, and why can't I keep a partner?

We meet people by living our lives. Those who are meant to come around will. This occurs when we function from our highest Joy. Every Conscious breath is an act of Self Love. If we have allowed ourselves to become so busy, that we have forgotten to breathe, then we have absolutely zero chance of fully connecting with someone else. Another person will never serve as an answer to our problems. Approaching relationships worried about 'losing' someone, we've already lost our Self. That which can be lost, was never ours to begin with. When connecting, regardless of the duration, do so out of Respect and Appreciation, not usury. Healing and authentic relating occur when we realize that there is Strength in our Openness. That Power is inseparable from Love.

Sleeping Our Way to the Top

"If one properly enters a state of meditation before sleeping, one's whole sleep is transformed."

- Osho[93]

According to the National Institute of Neurological Disorders and Stroke, approximately 40 million people in the United States suffer from chronic, long-term sleep disorders.[94] When we consider difficulty sleeping, this has been estimated to be as high as 70 million.[95] Further, over 4% of the U.S. population 'require' prescription medication in order to fall asleep; and that doesn't even include those using over the counter relief, drugs, and/or alcohol.[96] All of this, just to perform a necessary and natural bodily function. *The mind's catheter.*

Sleep is required for a balanced, healthy Life. It returns us to our natural state of Nothingness. About 9 years ago, I was frustrated that there wasn't enough 'time' in the day, so began experimenting with my sleep. I learned that navy personnel will sleep/work in 4/8 hour shifts when on duty. This meant sleeping from midnight to 4 am, working until noon, sleeping until 4 pm, and then working again until midnight. Unfortunately, I kept missing that second sleep cycle. Next, I experimented sleeping four hours a day, with a thirty minute nap. Eventually, this took a toll. After years of experimenting, I found 6-8 hours of daily sleep provides for optimal holistic performance. That being said, we are all unique and have our own preferences. Regardless of the duration, deep sleep is a must.

How to Sleep Better

1. Examine our daily choices (food, activity, inactivity, goals, etc.), and assess if they are in alignment with being the best version of our Self.

2. Exercising the body to physical exhaustion will encourage sleep.

    a. We need not go overboard. Daily exercise to the point of sweating will usually suffice.

    b. Check out Jeff Cavaliere's YouTube channel, Athlean-X, for more information on exercising.

3. Stretching before bed.

4. Fifteen minutes of reading prior to bed.

5. Fifteen minutes of meditation before falling asleep.

    a. The slow breathing or Witnessing meditations listed in the Appendix will be of benefit.

6. Create a list of daily tasks. This allows us to let go of what needs to be done tomorrow. We can sleep relaxed, knowing everything will be waiting for us when we awake. Cross items off the list as they're completed. Celebrate the victories. *All work and no play makes Jack something something.*

7. Do at least ONE thing that is in furtherance of a passion or goal for the day. This will provide a sense of accomplishment and fulfillment like no other.

8. Napoleon Hill suggests programming our subconscious mind prior to falling asleep.[97] The last thing we think about before we fall asleep programs our subconscious mind. It will bring the desired outcome(s) to the forefront of Consciousness (our waking Life). Ever go to bed Grateful for something and then find more of it the next day?

Say it with Your Chest

"The spine is the highway to the Infinite. Your own body is the temple of God. It is within your own self that God must be realized."

- Paramahansa Yogananda[98]

Although often overlooked, posture serves a significant factor in affecting our holistic Health. How we stand and walk can speak volumes about our mental, physical, emotional, and spiritual dispositions. Ergonomics aside, our posture even shows itself in how we sit. Good posture communicates self-confidence. It's not what we say, it's how we say it. Good posture speaks volumes well before a single word is uttered. Due to constant cell phone use, and restrictive work environments (often requiring sitting for long periods of time), many people find their spine in misalignment. This contributes to slumped shoulders and lower back pain. Over time, a misaligned spine can cause nerve damage, and lead to even more severe, debilitating injuries.

Chiropractors and masseuses are highly recommended when within budget. If not, see if there's things that can be substituted. For instance, junk food or eating out six days a week. A foam roller is beneficial in breaking up fibromyalgia (a vibrating foam roller is even better). Until properly broken down, this serves as an ever tightening vice grip on our muscles. Daily stretching will lengthen and strengthen our muscles. This serves to prevent, and sometimes even correct, deformities in posture. Stretching the following areas will have a profound impact on our posture: chest, shoulders, back, neck, spine, groin, hamstrings, quads, calves, achilleas, hip flexors, and abductors.

A Couple Tips on Preventing or Correcting Poor Posture:

1. Keep the head and chin up. Eyes forward.

    a. If using a cell phone. Raise the hands to face height, rather than slumping forward and dropping our head.

2. Stand straight up with the chest out. Big chest. Show the world your chest.

3. Shoulders back. This will naturally occur when the chest is broadened.

4. Allow the lower back to arch to its natural curvature while standing tall.

5. Hang for a minimum of two minutes a day from a pull up bar.

    a. If needed, break this up into 30 second intervals. If this is still too difficult to begin with, stand on a stool and bend the knees to get the hands accustomed to handling this weight. Joe Rogan describes the importance of hanging in greater depth here.[99]

I'll Give Ya a Hundred Grand to Cut Off Your Arm

"Training gives us an outlet for suppressed energies created by stress and thus tones the spirit just as exercise conditions the body."

- Arnold Schwarzenegger[100]

When walking a spiritual path, it is easy to forget our feet touching the ground. Money, clothing, and other material possessions often lose all appeal, beyond survival and convenience. Our body is our temple. A vehicle for our Consciousness to experience this plane. To enjoy, sense, and play with Life. It has entered a short-term lease agreement with Mother Earth. If our bodies were a car rental, we'd have to get a second job to cover the cost of the damage when we returned it. "Well sir, the interior's destroyed, and it will not pass a smog test. But don't worry, it'll likely never run again given the copious amounts of sugar we found in its gas tank." *Hahah, man, I'm gonna get dinged for that.* Movement is medicine. If we're healthy, we're happy. Plain and simple. Continuously becoming the best version of our Self is not a vanity, it is the epitome of Self-Love.

As has been discussed, God is always speaking, we just gotta listen. A couple of months ago, my friend and I were parking the cart after a round of golf. Before our feet touched the ground, we were greeted by Ed, sixty years old and full of Life. He had a grip that would crush a coconut, and a personality that'd knock it off the tree. Echoing our conversation on the course, Ed spoke on the importance of taking care of our bodies. He impersonated comedian/actor Norm McDonald harassing a friend who was overweight.

Norm offered his friend a hundred grand to cut off his leg. He turned it down, so Norm upped it to a million. The friend could even stop just below the knee! No chance. Norm then requested a quote for the arm. The friend wasn't having it. After establishing that he valued his body, Norm inquired why then doesn't he take better care of it. If he's not willing to trade an arm or a leg for a million bucks, why give it away for a couple of candy bars and a can of pop?

Most of us aren't willing to chop off a limb for a million dollars (although recent research by Duke University Medical Center suggests humans do possess, to a lesser degree, regenerative capabilities similar to that of salamanders and zebrafish[101]). So why do we choose to inhale, ingest, and inject unhealthy substances into our body? Usually because the effects are not so immediate. We can eat that cake, drink that liquor, fry that bread, smoke those cigarettes, or substitute stretching with scratching; and a limb will not suddenly fall off. However, it will take a toll over time.

We Can't Outwork Poor Nutrition Habits[102]

According to the National Center for Health Statistics, nearly 70% of adults, and 17% of children (2-19 years), in the United States are overweight or obese.[103] High stress, lack of exercise, and poor nutritional choices are the primary ingredients feeding this trend. People often overeat in an attempt to feel full. Really, this fullness sought is a desire to feel Love. Food will never replace LOVE, so people continue overeating. This overcompensation reflects a wound.

According to Harvard Medical School, people will eat what is in front of them, even if full and they know it is not good for them.[104] Therefore, make it as easy as possible to eat healthy. Have fresh fruits and vegetables just as convenient to access as a bag of potato chips. Investigate the acidity and alkalinity of these foods, and seek to balance the body's pH towards alkaline. An alkaline diet increases Health, and reduces morbidity and mortality from chronic diseases.[105] Healthy eating habits contribute significantly to our holistic Health and optimal function.

When creating a meal plan, choose foods that are not only healthy, but that also taste good. Guarantee there's plenty of options out there for everyone. Stic Man of Dead Prez has said, healthy food "is costly, but being sick is more expensive."[106] Cutting out gluten, starches, unhealthy sugars (such as, but not limited to, aspartame and high fructose corn syrup), as well as processed foods is a great start. A couple of quick google searches for superfoods will provide a strong platform to build a plan catered to our liking. Give it twenty-two days, and I can promise we'll never want to go back.

A Basic Formula for Weight

Recently, a Health coach and several personal trainers shared a simple formula for altering (increasing or reducing) our weight. I have found it helpful, and it follows:

> If trying to gain weight, multiply your caloric intake by 20. If losing weight, multiply by 15. Let's use an example for gaining weight. I want to weigh 165 lbs. Therefore, I would multiple 165 x 20, and this is the amount of healthy calories I will consume daily. I will further consume 165 grams of protein to sustain this weight.

The Health of our bodies are not determined solely by our calorie and protein intake. Not even close. Fats, vitamins, minerals, fibers, and nutrients serve a powerful influence as well. The cleaner we eat (unprocessed foods such as, but not limited to: fruits, vegetables, seeds, nuts, and fish) the healthier and more coherent our mind and body feel. We are what we eat. Kinda gives a new perspective on assholes in this world don't it?

The Power of Intention on our Food

"Hippocrates said that your medicine should be your food, or your food should be your medicine."

- Dr. Sebi[107]

Everything in Existence carries a vibrational frequency. How the food was prepared will have a significant impact on the quality of its sustenance. Food prepared with Love will serve a tremendous benefit to the recipient. If a meal was prepared in haste, with anger, or by an individual in a negative mood; it would be better to go hungry. We are not consuming 'food', we're utilizing all the Energy that went into producing it. Do not trade convenience for quality.

In double and triple blind studies, Dr. Emoto and colleagues have tested the effects of intention on the aesthetic crystallization of water molecules. The studies found that people located in Japan, Germany, and Australia were able to positively influence the appearance of water crystals. A large panel of independent judges assessed the appearance of each water crystal, rating its 'beauty' based on several qualifying factors.[108] Dr. Emoto has also demonstrated that harmonious thoughts, words, and music will positively impact the aesthetics of water crystals.[109] Whereas, discord and negativity (playing heavy metal music for example), produced grave mutation and asymmetry. These water crystals were described as 'ugly'. Bear in mind, depending on age, the human body is composed of 70-90% water.[110] Dr. Emoto's research inspires great insight into the Power of prayer and Gratitude prior to eating.

The Fast Track to a Slow Day

My experience with fasting has taught me that eating often occurs out of habit. That hunger begins in the mind, and if we pay close enough attention, the body is completely satiated. Recent trends, athletes, and many medical professionals have promoted the use of intermittent fasting. Here, a portion of the day is dedicated to eating, while for the remainder of the day, the body processes that food. These methods are suggested to better utilize the food's nutrients, while burning more of the body's stored and unnecessary fat. This is further suggested to strengthen the organs, by allowing them to rest for greater periods of time (versus constantly breaking down and processing food). When the body is functioning from optimal, stored nutrition levels, intermittent and alternate day fasting, have demonstrated the following results: a reduction in body fat and blood pressure; as well as, but not limited to, the reversal of malady (for example, diabetes, Parkinson's and cancer).[111] Feeding the face, need not be limited to matters of food. It is all the ways in which we seek sustenance for our attachments.

Extended periods of water fasting (say 72 hours), have demonstrated improved neuro, cognitive, and physiological functioning.[112] If desiring to engage in a fast, it is important to understand why, and prepare accordingly. Also, as a disclosure, consult with a doctor. There, I've done my due diligence. Personally, prior to engaging in a three-day water fast, I had been intermittent fasting for about three months. I stocked up on omega fatty acids, zincs, and other vitamins and minerals prior to the fast. I exercised with weights throughout the entire fast. I gained muscle, yet did not notice a significant decrease in body fat (although there were many variables affecting that measurement). However, it is reported that people often do. When breaking any extended fast, it is vital to understand that we are resetting our body's chemistry. Training it on how to process food again. Therefore, I highly recommend doing a lot of research prior to beginning, and/or ending a fast. If it becomes harmful to the body, cease immediately.[113]

When fasting, go about the day as normal. Meditate, work, exercise, socialize, engage in whatever would normally be done for that day. Let this be an opportunity to become more Aware of our connection with GOD. To Feel and breathe this Energy flowing through our bodies. There is no need to tell everyone of our 'starvation' and *incredible feat*. Osho suggests to let fasting be a cultivation of greater Awareness.[114]

Strengthening Our Body

I am not a personal trainer. As a disclaimer, consult with a professional for guidance prior to beginning an exercise program. Obviously, if you have a medical condition, speak with a doctor before participating in any physical activity. Again, I highly recommend checking out Athlean-X, a YouTube channel by Jeff Cavaliere. This is by far one of the best resources I have found for, as he puts it, "science-based training."

Many of us become discouraged because we don't see results immediately. We may be trying to lose weight and actually gain a pound, forgetting that muscle weighs more than fat. There's days we fall. That happens, and that's ok. However, there's no such thing as stagnation. We're either moving forward or backwards. Whichever direction, none of that stops us from choosing to do something for our benefit right now. Even if we pissed the whole day away, we can still do some sit ups or stretch before bed. Consistency and routines are necessary, but just making sure we get it in at some point in the day, is enough to begin creating positive changes in our Life.

Types of Exercise

Stretching and foam rolling are just as important as actual exercise in building a strong, functional, and healthy body. A gym is an excellent resource, but not essential for getting started. Weight and/or body weight training strengthen bone density, and serve to prevent typical ailments that can be associated with aging, such as: cellular health, hormonal imbalances, muscle reduction, and osteoporosis.[115] Compound exercises and lateral movements contribute to better

106

athleticism by developing Power, Strength, speed, agility, and balance. Prioritizing our core will serve to prevent injuries, while improving the overall functionality of our body. According to Jeff Cavaliere, a strong core will also serve to protect and maintain the integrity of our spine (basically performing the same function as a weight belt).[116] This includes all the abdominal muscles, hips, and lower back.

As with anything, developing the proper form is fundamental prior to adding Power and/or speed. Research the correct anatomical forms to each exercise, then begin light. If new to exercising, a few weeks of light training, will provide stability and build muscle memory. Whatever exercise we are engaging in, it is vital to place one's mind in the muscle throughout the full movement. Explore the Buddha Breath meditation discussed in the Appendix. Same principle. This unleashes our internal Power through the muscle(s).

Including various forms and intensity of cardio throughout the week will increase blood circulation, flexibility, and prevent excess fat from remaining on the body. Cardio is any exercise that increases the heart rate, while encouraging us to sweat. When we sweat, we release toxins from the body. Though no bed of roses, deodorant at the gym prevents the full release of these toxins. In a 20 year, longitudinal study of 2000 men in Finland, the researchers found that incorporating thirty minutes in a sauna three times per week, demonstrated a 24% reduction in high blood pressure, as well as massive reductions in mortality and memory disease.[117]

Women and men naturally have different body types. Our polarity contributes to our attraction. Workout plans will vary based upon the desired outcome. Different objectives require varying courses of action. Decide what the best version and expression of Self looks like, and more importantly, feels like, then go for it. It is important to hold our Self accountable. No one else is keeping score. We know when we've done our best, and we know when we had more to give. Make adjustments when needed, knowing consistency will always surpass intensity. As Nipsey Hussle gently reminded us, "instead of trying to build a brick wall, lay a brick every day. Eventually, you'll look up and have a brick wall."[118] #Marathon

Laughing in the Face of Danger

"Laughter is a moment when we are completely ourselves."

- George Carlin[119]

Edgar Cayce reminded us that, "whatever the disturbance, do not lose the sense of humor, but be patient."[120] It has been said that laughter is the best medicine. Looking at the world of comedy, we find this exemplified. Many of the topics addressed by comedians are of no laughing matter. However, through artful spin, the comedian finds a way to bring humor to the situation. Often by pointing out the absurdity of the phenomenon.

Laughter has demonstrated significant positive effects on an individual's psychological, emotional, and physiological Health. For instance, Saranne Rothberg and Norman Cousins were each diagnosed with terminal illnesses. Both individuals cited daily laughter as pivotal in their recoveries.[121] Growing up, I always heard, "don't sweat the small stuff." Making it a point to laugh at that which is out of our control, actually brings back a sense of control. We may not always be able to dictate or predict what will happen to us, but we can always choose how we go from there. Research has demonstrated that laughing has many psychological and physiological benefits, such as: reduced stress, increased oxygen, improved blood circulation, a strengthened immune system, the release of endorphins, anti-aging properties, enhanced brain health, and, but not limited to, enriched social connections.[122]

Sometimes it's laugh or cry. Both have a place and serve their purpose. We need to vent. There is nothing 'wrong' with that. Just don't take it out on anybody else. If isolation and a quiet space are needed, create it, then let loose. The catharsis will be rejuvenating. Now, breaking down into uncontrollable sobbing may not always be the best route. Why not laugh it off? Look for the silver lining and find the humor in it. We don't need to put on a show for anyone. This is about us, and our perspective. It may be as small as a smirk, or have us looking for a change of drawers. The point is to allow ourselves to be natural. It's our choice to find the humor in Life.

Obviously, some moments in Life are pretty hard to laugh at. The loss of a child for example. There is nothing funny about this. However, once this moment has passed, it may be healing to laugh here and there in remembrance of the good times that were had. As I mentioned in the chapter on death, I have Family Friends that lost a Loved one unexpectedly when she was young. The pain is still there, guaranteed. But the laughter reminds us of her Joy and zest for Life. There are plenty of stories to recall of her having Dad wrapped around her finger, conspiring with Mom, or duping her Brother just for the fun of it. The body has been returned to Mother Earth, but the memories are our Souls' to keep.

Daily Laughter

1. Set aside at least ten minutes a day to laugh.

2. Choose a comedy, new or old, that will have us asking, "where'd my ass go?"

    a. Nowadays, we can find nearly anything we want on YouTube or through streaming. Something that has us laughing so hard our stomach hurts, and/or we have tears rolling down our cheeks, will immediately improve our mental, emotional, and physical Health.

Take Two Walks in Nature and Call Me in the Morning

"In every walk with nature one receives far more than [she or] he seeks."

- John Muir[123]

D o not look at nature as separate from IT. All that can be learned, can be learned from nature. The cycles and rhythms. Collaboration and survival. Competition. Adaptation and extinction. The absolute necessity of a moment to moment Awareness. It is one breeze that graces this Earth's atmosphere. One ocean that tides the shores of every continent. Each region just has a different name for it. Continents, though really nothing more than large islands, are all still connected at the Earth's mantle.

The Earth is vast and beautiful. Every step is the blaze of a new trail. Connecting with nature is good for our Health. The sights, sounds, and smells have a positive effect on our biopsychosocial well-being. This includes, but is not limited to: improved short-term memory, restored mental energy, stress relief, reduced inflammation, better vision, improved concentration, sharper thinking, expanded creativity, improved mental health, a strengthened immune system, reduced risk of early death, and possible anti-cancer effects.[124]

It's no coincidence that pleasant individuals and new experiences are regarded as a 'breath of fresh air'. The mind and body become imbued by nature's exuberance. Jumping in the ocean cleanses and

112

recharges the body; improving the skin, immune system, and, but not limited to, circulation.[125] Climbing mountains widens one's perspective. Walking, breathing, and bathing in the richness of a forest, the body absorbs helpful microbes (in Japan, when combined with techniques in mindfulness, this is regarded as shinrin-yoku).[126] Traversing the desert, one is reminded of yesterday's rain forests.[127] Kayaking in untamed rivers, one learns very quickly the futility of fighting the natural flow of Life. Nature is Free from judgments, expectations, rules, morality, and boundaries. The drop contains the ocean. The sky harbors the stars. As with nature, so it is with us.

Vessels for Healing

"It is not I who Heals. It Is God."

~ John of GOD[128]

T he medical system in the United States is in dire need of reform. Cost has made access to this system and its medical advances difficult and divisive amongst the population. In 2012, over 54 million people in the U.S. lived in families who had difficulty paying medical bills, often resulting in the foregoing of treatment.[129] Even in countries that provide socialized medical services to their populace, residents still tout a need for improvement.[130]

The treatment of most ailments through 'western' medicine requires the patient to procure an outside variable. For instance, the ingestion of a pill, an operation performed by a physician, therapeutic counseling, et cetera. What if we had the ability to heal ourselves? What would this mean for the individual and our societal infrastructure? How would this affect the advancement of our species? For thousands of years, sages have guided us that we must go within to remedy an illness.

Many modalities exist outside of 'western' medicine that serve to heal. Oftentimes, these approaches incorporate a greater holistic examination of the individual. This includes their mental, physical, emotional, sexual, economic, and spiritual Health. Some of these modalities include, but are not limited to, Tantra, Qi Gong, Tai Chi,

Reiki, acupuncture, sound healing, and Lightwork. Barbara Brennan, Edgar Cayce, and John of God have been recognized worldwide for their work.

Understanding Ourselves as Vessels

Through Oneness, all becomes available. To heal, we do not ignore a malady and hope it goes away. We acknowledge, accept, and take appropriate action. Oneness is realized when we stop the chase, cease the search, and just melt into what IS. The deeper we melt into our Peace (The Oneness), the better prepared we are to serve as vessels for healing. There is nowhere in existence where GOD does not exist. LOVE is what heals. It is our very nature. Everything else is just forgetfulness. We are merely serving as vessels, and need only get out of the way for this Divine Intelligence to work its magic.

My Experiences as a Vessel

I have practiced Energy Bodywork publicly since 2014. Since that time, the experiences have been incredible. For instance, one person was released from the hospital after being bedridden with stomach parasites. Scar tissue had fused another woman's uterus to her abdominal wall. After the session, an ultrasound revealed that this had completely vanished. Many women have experienced thousands of orgasms flooding their bodies during the sessions. Others have been engulfed in Light, reconnected into their Peace, received messages, or reconciled trauma. One client described it as years of intense psychotherapy, rolled into a two-hour session. Some have even found relief from constant migraines or food poisoning. These are just a couple examples of the countless blessings that have occurred.

While serving as a vessel for any healing, it's important to remember, that it is not "Chad" healing anybody. I am connecting with the Life Force Energy and getting 'out of the way'. This allows the Energy to flow through the person's body, as was originally intended. The deeper our Surrender, the greater our access to the Super Consciousness.

For instance, during one session, I was shown a picture of a white, boxy car. It looked old school, like from the 80's or early 90's. I didn't mention anything during the session, but after the debriefing it kept nagging me. Later that night, it was so overwhelming, I texted her, asking if a white boxy-looking car meant anything. She responded with a list of cars she had driven. The first one I googled was the vehicle I was shown. I sent a picture back. "Oh my God! That used to be my Parents' car. I used to steal that and go down to TJ with it. Oh God, the things I used to do in it! I should've died so many times!" During the session, the vehicle appeared in her throat chakra, which is associated with speaking our Truth.

Again, this is just one of countless examples. The point I would really like to drive home is that all of us serve as vessels for the Divine. It is within each of us. By shedding the layers of our identifications, attachments, judgments, and expectations we can 'get out of the way' and let this Life Force Energy flow through us. This Energy is creative, healing, and orgasmic; here for all of us to tap into at any time. It is our choice whether or not we do so.

FAITH & GRATITUDE

Patience is the Ultimate Faith

"The seed of the Chinese bamboo tree spends five years under the ground with no growth whatsoever. But in the fifth year, it grows over 80 feet tall in less than a month. Have a little Patience in Life. Your success might just be around the corner."

- Les Brown[131]

P atience and Faith walk hand in hand with God. Everyone who has ever hiked Everest, has done so one step at a time. Faith told them they could, Patience weathered the terrain. Faith not only conquers mountains, it heals (remember the chapter exploring placeboes?). It is following our gut, listening to our heart, sticking our neck out, and starting over when necessary. Patience is relentless, yet unattached. Knowing that all will unfold in Divine order.

On August 5, 2018, I had a dream. I wandered down a school hallway, finding a dirt bike parked between two lockers. An envelope rested snug between the handle bars and brake cable. "Faith" was handwritten on the front. After fighting and struggling for so long, I felt reassured that it was all worth it. Upon awakening, I kept this to myself. 'Faith through struggle' then appeared as the topic of our Sunday morning Prayer. Excitement built for what was to come. That afternoon, on a bike ride to the gym, my front tire ran over a piece of

117

paper. I doubled back into the busy intersection to confirm my suspicions. At the top of the page, "Faith" was centered in bold.

My Walk in Faith

For me, Faith has been leaving with a thousand dollars to backpack Europe and Asia for a year. Taking that first step off of the plane in a foreign land. No idea where I'm going, or how I'm going to get there, but knowing in my heart that I have to move forward. Faith has been getting myself stuck on the side of a mountain, in the middle of the night, with a helicopter looking for me. Knowing that signaling them would cause a rockslide due to the loose, enormous boulders teetering above my head. Faith was slamming my foot into a cactus (with sandals on), hugging the wall, and inching my way twenty feet across a ledge no bigger than the width of my foot. For me, Faith has been sleeping in bushes to try and gain an understanding of what it felt like to live on the streets. Faith has been having no job, and walking ten to twenty miles a day in Japan until I found one (also not speaking Japanese at the time). For me, Faith was being so hungry that I began blacking out and seeing spots, feeling the acid in my stomach eat away at my insides. Faith has been knowing that I would be fine and make it through all of this.

Before continuing, I have been blessed with the Love and support of my family and friends throughout my entire Life. Had they not been there, I would have still continued on my heart's path, but I can promise, it would have looked very different. Guaranteed. I am forever Grateful and there's no way to repay them for all they have done.

Since 2007, I have more or less, worked for my Self. I have begun several businesses, and taken side jobs when things were slow. I have built and sold bikes for a friend, moved homes, painted houses, taught kids, dug trenches, ripped out decks, relocated trees, chopped firewood, and taken a sledge hammer and pick axe to boulders in a field full of poison oak. That last job wasn't so great on my profit margin…or sex Life. It's alright. My Father-in-Law, and everyone else thought it was hilarious too. When a last minute business opportunity presented itself down in Rosarito, Mexico, I didn't have enough money to even buy a stamp. I agreed to the meeting, then grabbed my bike, a pair of gloves, a broom, and a couple of garbage bags. That morning was spent jumping in and out of dumpsters collecting recyclables for enough cash to make it down there.

Aside from family, friends, and side jobs; I have utilized student loans to subsidize my cost of living while building my businesses. The large amount owed after graduation, doesn't even include the undergrad my Parents so Lovingly paid for. This has been my expression of Faith. I have considered these loans to be an investment in me. A betting on my success. A knowing of what's to come, then working relentlessly for it.

Our Walk in Faith

"Take the first step in Faith. You don't have to see the whole staircase, just take the first step."

- Dr. Martin Luther King Jr.

We need not go to such extremes to subsidize our cost of living, or walk in Faith, but a willingness to do what it takes to survive, while still being true to our hearts, is an absolute must. The staircase may wind, creak, and crack. However, we only need to navigate it one stair at a time. Faith directs our path. Patience lightens the load.

Questions:

1. What has beckoned at my Soul?

   _____

2. How would I feel if I express, share, or achieve this?

   _____

3. Why do I want this?

   _____

4. What does success look like when I picture it?

   _____

5. What is preventing me from doing something right now?

   _____

6. If I were to spend a little time every day working on this, where would I start?

   _____

7. What skills do I need to learn? What can I do right now with what I have?

   _____

8. What's the first thing I can do? What's the next, and the one after that?

   _____

Practicing Gratitude in a World Full of Suffering

"Are you ready for the real revolution? Which is the evolution of the mind. If you seek, then you Shall find, that we all grew from the Divine."

- Flava Flav of Public Enemy, in "He Got Game" title song from the movie soundtrack[132]

Life happens, tragedies strike, and stress pulls us in forty different directions. We can find ourselves, or our Loved ones, in horrible circumstances at the blink of an eye. Simply turning on a television, and paying attention to the socioeconomic plight of our planet, will provide great justification as to why we can't be happy this very moment. A part of us may even feel guilty for wanting to do so. *There's so much to do.*

The Sentiment of Many

As the roaring beach fire faded to a crackle, we knew the evening to our first date was soon to follow. An unexpected discussion into the intricacies of Life, led her to fight back tears. "There's just so much hate, greed, and violence. Ignorance, poverty, and intolerance. What do I do?! Do I take the ostrich approach and just ignore it? Do I try and forget that I'm aware of it, or do I spend my whole Life fighting it? What do I do?!" My heart had never felt more understood.

Grandad on the Boondocks once advised Huey, "we do our best." As someone who had dedicated much of his waking Life after twenty-five to 'fighting the system', it became apparent that I first needed to work on myself. It was essential to understand where I was demonstrating these undesirable qualities in my Life. As such, the world around me began to change. We can focus on Gratitude or atrocity, both are a choice. The best time to start practicing Gratitude is right now.

Clinical studies indicate that the practice of Gratitude can: lower blood pressure, improve immune function, promote happiness and well-being, encourage generosity, and inspire cooperation; while reducing the risk of depression, anxiety, and substance abuse disorders.[133] There is always something to Appreciate and be Grateful for. Let the first thoughts of our day be that of Appreciation. In this Life, momentum serves a valuable role in the manifestation (rather, realization) of our physical reality. It takes far greater effort to redirect negative momentum, than it does to keep positive Energy going.

grATTITUDE

To reiterate, Life is a constant Prayer. It's not what we do, it's how we do it. There's a theme to this book. When working, it has always been helpful for me to find the Joy in whatever it is that I am doing. For instance, even if digging a ditch, I can still be Grateful. *This is such great exercise. I Love being outside in nature. Look at how much progress I've made. What a blessing to have a body that can perform such manual labor! This is great warrior training.* If that ditch is not dug, then I do not eat or pay my rent. I don't care if it's raining or the ground's frozen, the work will be done. *What's your dirt doing in my hole Luke? I'm moving it boss.*

It is our choice how that occurs. We can groan throughout the whole process (wasting precious moments of Life that we will never get back), or in Gratitude, we can find the Joy and beauty in every swing of the pick ax and sledge hammer. Our Health and work will reflect our choices. Our pay will eventually echo our attitude. If working with a partner or on a team, whatever attitude we choose will influence that of our teammate(s). The quality of work will be reflected in the final product.

Letting Go

I have found that the more we let go of attachments in Life, the more we have to be Grateful for. Anything can serve as an attachment. This does not mean we have to relinquish all worldly possessions and seclude to the Himalayas (although, I do hear it's beautiful this time of year). No. It simply means becoming Aware of what we are attached to. How does this affect our Life? What would happen if we did not 'possess' this anymore? Would we still be happy or Grateful? Could we?

I know every time I have broken a bone or fallen ill, it has made me Appreciate my Health that much greater. I once lost the use of my right hand (which had been my predominate hand), for well over a year before receiving a surgery. I broke my wrist, dislocated it, and ripped a tendon in half. I did not have medical insurance, so I kept working. Taping it up and hoping it would get better over time. It popped out of place about 10 times a day, for a year. Every time it hurt just as bad as the first. I felt the tendon roll up into the elbow. Eventually, I qualified for Medicare and began my search for a surgeon. Many doctors refused to treat me. The first doctor who agreed, proposed amputating my arm up to the elbow. He said it'd be easier, and my chance for a successful recovery had already passed. Where I was spiritually at that time, if he was younger, I would have beaten him senseless with the nub. Eventually, I was blessed and guided to Dr. Mann, out of Escondido. A wonderful surgeon who was kind and confident in my recovery. The rehabilitation was not easy. There came a point where I told my wrist, "you will bend, or I will break you off." I'm blessed to say that today, I'm stronger than ever and in the best shape of my Life. Every day is an opportunity to improve upon yesterday.

Learn from yesterday

Plan for tomorrow

Live/breathe right now

Even moments such as these offer their own beauty and opportunity for Gratitude. How's the story go? I used to complain about having no shoes, until I met a man with no legs. It should be noted, the person with no legs, was happy and Grateful as can be to still have hands and arms to drag himself around.

Suggestions for Practicing Gratitude:

1. Do without from time to time. This need not be masochistic. Use this as an opportunity to increase our Appreciation for what is available to us right now. This can range from putting

our phones away for the day, washing with only cold water, taking public transit (if we already have a vehicle), putting a blind fold on for periods of time while in the house (if we are blessed to already have the use of our eyes or a house), ear plugs, or sleeping outside. We need not put ourselves in danger to Appreciate this moment, but it is important to sometimes remind our Self of how good we really do have it.

2. Begin every day by giving thanks for being alive. The breath in our body, our body, our senses, and so on. Tony Robbins begins his day, prior to even stepping foot out of bed, by giving thanks for three things in his Life. He starts big (family, friends, Health, the sun, etc.) and then hones in from there.[134]

3. Give thanks before eating and going to bed.

4. When situations of discord arrive, give thanks for their occurrence, then see how quickly we are able to bring our Self back to a state/vibration of Gratitude. Again, start big then begin honing in.

5. Throughout the day, make it a practice to see how much we can be Grateful for. When walking, sitting, driving, talking, listening, working, making Love, whatever. Every moment offers something.

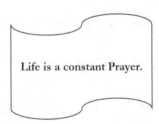

Life is a constant Prayer.

LOVE

Instant Karma, Add Two Scoops and Stir

🎼 *"Instant Karma's gonna get you. Gonna look you right in the face. Better get yourself together darlin'. Join the human race."*

- John Lennon, "Instant Karma (We All Shine On)"[135]

Life has a way of unfolding for the best. The Law of Karma is often discredited by citing the countless atrocities that have occurred on our planet. Understandably so. No human being, from the perspective of a lifetime, deserves to suffer as millions have upon this Earth. Wars, genocides, famines, oppression, sexual abuse, mutilations, terminal illness, the list is ad infinitum. Karma does not belittle the suffering of 'others'. It is a reminder to accept where we are for the moment, and make the best of right now.

As the evidence from near death experiences, and readings from individuals such as Edgar Cayce have highlighted, Consciousness does not exist in one lifetime. It takes Infinite forms through Time and Space. All existing simultaneously in this Singularity. This is not a ticket to apathetically gawk at the suffering of our Sisters and Brothers. If we are in a position to help, we do. Every breath is an opportunity to Love.

One Day at the Recycling Center...

As we were closing the yard for the day, a young man barreled down Fourteenth Avenue on his BMX bike. He jumped the sidewalk and ditched the bike all in one motion. Lunging for the fence, he begged us to take one more customer. This wasn't that out of the ordinary. Every day it felt like we were asked to reopen for one more person. If we could make an exception, we would. We understood this may be their only cash for the remainder of the evening. However, that day we had already closed the doors, shut down the computers, and locked away the scale and bins. We didn't have many options at that point, and calmly explained this. He screamed and cursed, chucking glass bottles at us from across the parking lot. This went on for a good minute, when he suddenly stopped. Lost in his fit of rage, someone stole his remaining two bags of recycling, and his bike! We may not be able to escape any past Karma owed, but that doesn't mean we need to create any further debts.

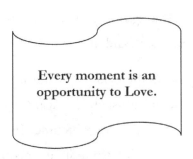

Every moment is an opportunity to Love.

Forgiveness is not a Convenience

(Clint) "It's a hell of a thing killing a man. We take away all he's got, and all he's ever gonna have." (response from kid) "Yea, well I guess he had it coming." (Clint) "We all have it coming kid."

- Clint Eastwood, Unforgiven[136]

How dare we ask God to Love & Forgive us unconditionally, when we have yet to do the same. We are so quick to beg for Forgiveness when we are at fault. *Lord please Forgive me for I have 'sinned'.* Why then, do we treat it like our last dollar when it's time to hand it out? It's one thing to Forgive others after the fact. It's another to Forgive them in the midst of the act.

Being angry doesn't serve anyone. We are the ones left carrying the burden of its heavy load. The other person is fine. They could care less. We're not 'getting back at them'. I have heard Gautam Buddha described holding onto anger, as drinking poison…and expecting the other person to die.

Forgiveness and Acceptance are not judgment and submission, nor are they forgetfulness. We need not put ourselves in harm's way to prove a point. Lions are often cool with hyenas, until they get too familiar and have to be put in their place. Usually, when the hyenas go after the women or young. That happens once, and only once. When someone shows that they are willing to lie, steal, or cheat us; be gone. Mentally, emotionally, and/or physically abuse us; adios. Belittle us for

129

their own illusory sense of superiority and well-being, thank them, realize this is where they are in their spiritual journey; then why not whistle a little Willie Nelson as those feet brush up dirt on the road again. We need not surround our Self with that Energy. Although anything can be alchemized, if it serves no continual benefit, and the person doesn't demonstrate any effort to grow, bon voyage. It's not a 'no' to someone else, as much as it is a 'yes' to our Self. When we allow ourselves to partake in interactions that we know in our hearts are no good for us (jobs, relationships, and worst yet, thought processes), we end up serving as our own worst enemy.

Oftentimes, not only do we have a difficult time Forgiving 'others', we find it near impossible to Forgive our Self. Maybe we did something to someone that we shouldn't have, or said we'd do something, but didn't. If yesterday hadn't happened, we wouldn't be who we are today. If we wouldn't make the same choices at this moment, we've learned our lesson. Let the past be the past. It's over. Forgiveness lifts the veil darkening our room, and illuminates the shadows of our Soul. It is the Light of LOVE.

When it Comes to LOVE, We can do no Wrong

"If you Love a flower, don't pick it up. Because if you pick it up it dies and it ceases to be what you Love. So if you love a flower, let it be. Love is not about possession. Love is about Appreciation."

- Osho[137]

The Power of LOVE

People are eager to say "I Love You", but only upon contingency. If it's not parroted immediately, watch how quickly that sentiment changes. If "love" can be retracted as hastily as it has been offered, was it really Love?

How can we Love 'others' unconditionally, until we have first found this in our Self? Everyone, regardless of gender or creed, shares LOVE. We are bound by IT. IT belongs to no one. IT is not something that can be turned on or off. LOVE is beyond word, time, space, and face.

Distance is an illusion in all matters concerning the heart. We cannot escape LOVE. We can only build walls and imagine barriers, blinding us to that which we already are! GOD is LOVE. We are extensions of GOD. We are expressions of LOVE. Every single variation of Life is an extension and expression of GOD. Without exception. We have only been conditioned to forget, by those who have also forgotten.

As a humanity, we want to Love. We want to share Love, and be Loved. For this experience, we are willing to do anything for it. To leave no rock unturned, or planet unexplored. Forgetful that LOVE is our very Nature. IT is the air that sustains us. LOVE and breathing are synonymous. IT is the purpose of our very existence. Life is a continuous discovery of new ways to Love.

The Truth About Honesty

In this Universe filled with Infinite questions: LOVE is the only answer.

~ One LOVE. One GOD

It hurts to be lied to or feel taken advantage of. We often chalk it up to an innate, unchangeable fault in the other, or we stick around hoping our antagonist to have an epiphany. Perhaps we are willing to accept anything from our partner as long as she or he is Honest. This appears more than fair upon first glance, right? "Do whatever you want, just be Honest with me." What's so hard about that? However, this is a subtle act of control. It is the ego attempting to exert Power over another. This is still a far cry from LOVE. We are placing our values on another person and mandating they be followed to a T, or else.

What if we just live our Life and allow others to live theirs? If these lives meet up and coincide on the same vibe, great. Let's have fun together. If not, just as good. This isn't about 'freeing' that person. It's about Freeing our Self. Letting our Self off the hook. Freedom in this moment, gives us Freedom in every Moment.

132

Questions:

1. Where and when did I not Love myself (including childhood)? Why?

   _____

   _____

2. Am I still that same person, with the exact same mindset?

   _____

   _____

3. Who and/or what do I dislike? How will my Life change if I let this go?

   _____

   _____

4. The parts of me that I need to Love the most right now are:

   _____

   _____

5. I Love my Self for the following reasons:

   _____

   _____

FREEDOM

What's the Cost of Freedom?

𝄞 *"Emancipate yourself from mental slavery. None but ourselves can Free our mind."*

- Bob Marley, Redemption Song[138]

F ollowing our heart is Freedom. It is from here that dreams are realized. Illusions of fear and risk prevent us from living our dream. What are we willing to risk? What are we willing to lose? How much pain, isolation, and criticism are we willing to endure to see our dream through? To quote Tyler Durden in Fight Club, "the things we own, end up owning us [...] it's only after we've lost everything, that we're Free to do anything."[139]

Some are born with greater gifts and access to a wider range of resources. Looks, finances, athletic aptitude, artistic abilities, a discerning mind, and so on. However, it is the effort we exert developing our gifts into skills, that separates those living their dreams, from those still dreaming. There are plenty of people with an abundance of resources, living the Life prescribed as the 'American dream', who are still just flat out miserable. They travel, yet do not explore. They eat, but do not taste. Look, but have yet to see.

Those who dare to dream are often ridiculed or ostracized for expressing independent, creative thought. For simply asking, "Why?". When did we lose our ability to ask "Why"? Truthfully, we never lost it. Curious minds were muffled by distraction and busyness. Parents, though well intentioned, are often too mentally, emotionally, and physically exhausted paying bills, that on a sane planet, should not exist to begin with.[140]

Think about it. Who really has the authority to sell or rent us a piece of land? To build upon it? No façade of printed paper, or ones and zeros entered into a computer database, will ever demark a true ownership of any natural resource. That includes, but is not limited to, land, water, air, ingenuity, or Consciousness.

So does it take lots of money to live one's dreams? No. It helps, but it is not necessary. **Faith** is required. We have to be willing to give up everything. We have to be willing to suffer. We have to be willing to be hungry. We must be **Free** of attachments. This does not mean that we will suffer, or that we have to give up everything, but we must be willing. This is our commitment to our Self, and to GOD.

To live our dream we need to ask our Self:

1. What truly makes me Joyful?

2. What does my heart yearn to do every single day?

3. If money wasn't an issue, what would I want to do? How would I spend my time?

Can't You Live a 'Normal' Life like Everyone Else?

"Truth is the greatest protection we can have against any perceived threat on this plane."

- Shantam Nityama[141]

Testing Our Limits

It's difficult and hurts when those closest to us claim we are wasting our Life.

- "Why don't you get a *real* job?"

- "Why do you have to be so difficult?"

- "Don't you know the pain you're causing your family?"

- "We care about you and don't want to see you suffer."

- "Nobody wants to be with someone that's broke."

These are the moments that crack the bell. *Liberty.* Trials of Faith, fortitude, and commitment. Usually showing up at pivotal junctures. Our low points, just before the breakthrough. When doubt has sunk in, and the last ten ideas have come up short. Rent's due and we don't even have enough to mail the check. When we have the Courage to say this is what I'm doing with my Life, and I'm willing to die for it.

Living our dream begins with knowing our Self. Knowing who we came to this planet to be, and being it. Some will go to extremes to try

136

and convince us that we are not who we know we are. Let 'em. It has no bearing. Sometimes this is constructive and should be considered. Other times this comes from their insecurity. This will appear obvious when it becomes deliberately hurtful. No need to stick around. Keep going within and raising the vibration. Those who are meant to be there will remain. Those who are not, will simply fade away. No problems, grief, or hard feelings. No need to respond with defenses or match their rhetoric. All is an opportunity for Peace and Gratitude.

Everybody Knows What's Best for You

Living our dreams has nothing to do with 'proving' something to someone. Many choose to ride the bench in Life because of fear. A fear of failure, disappointment, or hardship. The uncertainty of stepping into the world. Of being violated or killed. Every day the media reinforces a belief in the inevitability of these threats. *The world is dangerous. Stay home! We'll let you know when it's safe again.* The appointed 'savior' need not always don a cross. Sometimes that person may sport a suit, robe, or uniform. Being led to believe that another has our best interest in mind, we play the role of subservient victim. Outsourcing Freedom, personal responsibility, and human rights for the promise of protection.

We have been led to believe that the best way to secure and protect our sovereignty is by electing 'officials'. These people are touted as capable 'experts', certain as to what's best for us. Let's examine this for a moment. Look at the people who proffer themselves 'leaders'. If it came down to it, how well would any one of these 'leaders' really do in a fight? What are their chances of survival in the woods or desert given limited resources? *Bear Grills 2020!* Most even have other people protecting them! Maybe the body guards should run the 'country'. We find ourselves in a sad state of affairs when we seek 'protection' from those who do not give a damn about us. They are not 'leaders', and they certainly are not 'advisors'. *When so and so gets elected to office, then we'll be on the right track. They can make it good again.* Seeking, begging, or demanding a better Life from someone else, is a surefire way to find ourselves under the tyranny of their rule.

We Must Be Able to Defend Our Self

"Only individuals who know themselves are sovereigns."

- Osho[142]

Plato suggests that a true leader has a Love for knowledge, and is able to physically defend oneself if needed.[143] Learning a martial art or fighting style will build confidence to move Freely about this planet. Even a few simple moves, can be enough to save one's Life. The human body is incredibly Powerful, yet vulnerable. When we learn how to fight, rarely will we have to.

Even our pheromones smell differently on the subtle level. This applies to most mammals in the animal kingdom. Sweat samples taken under various environmental conditions will produce a different smell for each situation (i.e. sex, excitement, anger, fear, joy). This registers in, and activates, varying regions of the brain.[144] For instance, sweat released through panic or anxiety will have a completely different smell from that released through sex or exercise. Amongst animals and humans, fear is often interpreted as a sign of weakness and vulnerability. People causing trouble usually seek out individuals that are easy targets. This means, someone smelling of fear and therefore less likely to retaliate with effective force.

Learning how to fight does not mean we engage in every confrontation. We should never antagonize a verbal conflict into a physical altercation as an excuse to 'defend' our Self. When two people fight a battle, both lose the war. If someone insults 'me' that is one thing. Ultimately, who is really even being insulted? Was anyone actually harmed? However, if someone poses a threat to the immediate safety of my Self or a Loved one, that is another story. Know Thy Self, and we shall know Freedom. Herein lies our Power. This is our Divine Nature.

Real Life Superheroes

At nineteen years old, Charlotte Heffeimire lifted a burning truck off of her Father.[145] Ms. Heffeimire, though absolutely amazing, is not unique in this regard. Individuals all over the globe are able to summon superhuman Strength during times of need. The moment is so engrossing, fear never had a chance to register and instigate doubt.

Author Authenticity

"A musician must make music, an artist must paint, a poet must write, if he is to be ultimately at Peace with himself. What a man can be, he must be."

- Abraham Maslow[146]

Being real and authentic is one of the simplest, yet most complex feats in a world that promotes plasticity. Look a certain way. Speak in a particular manner. Social etiquette and moral guidelines are purported as educational requirements for the 'civilized'. We aspire to average, and scour the Earth for validation…but to who's standards?! We even ask others to certify the legitimacy of a birth! Every fingerprint is unique for a reason.

So what are some things that make us unique? First and foremost, each of us came to this planet with a purpose. It need not be grandiose. Ultimately, there's no such thing anyways. Let's stop putting so much pressure on ourselves to 'prove' something. If we're authentic, our body will let us know. Our heart knows when our action (or inaction) is in alignment with our Highest Self. Contributing to, or expressing, our highest good. We all have preferences, and the sooner we speak our Truth, the better it is for everyone involved.

For instance, looking outside the societal influences that may manipulate our thoughts (desires) and behaviors (actions), some people genuinely want a monogamous relationship. While others

140

would be happiest openly and honestly relating with multiple partners. Life does not come pre-packaged. We often enter 'relationships' (which the term alone already carries bias and limiting belief systems minimizing any chance of an authentic interaction) with an idea of acquiescence.

Authentic relating extends well-beyond romantic encounters. In any interaction, we need not succumb to another's conduct to avoid conflict. The threat of confrontation can often subdue people into passivity. We may go silent, laugh nervously, or change the topic quickly. Leaving the encounter, a part of our Soul feels abused and betrayed. *I don't believe that! Why didn't I speak up and say something? Ah, well, I got too much going to get into an argument.*

Disagreement need not lead to argument. Napoleon Hill advises that people will often prove themselves wrong, just by remembering to ask them five simple words, "how do you know that?"[147] This phrase is a jack hammer chipping away at a foundation of lies. Peace can be maintained, while the individual is left with much to reflect upon. If the person is fascist in their approach, we always have the option of simply saying, "I don't agree with you on this subject, and I feel you'd benefit from looking deeper into it before stating such an opinion", and then walking away knowing we spoke our Truth.

Matthew 10:16 advises to be wise as a serpent, and harmless as a dove. Authentic living does not seek to change the thought patterns or habits of others. Nor does it place ourselves in unnecessary dangers. Authenticity is Aware of time and place, and moves accordingly. Each moment is new. One expression may be completely appropriate one moment, and its absolute contradiction in another. Loving 'others' and remembering they are where they are right now for a reason, takes the pressure out of feeling like we have to get a point across, or 'save' someone. As Ziggy Marley said, "I don't condemn, I don't convert."[148] Love is our religion, and Life is its Prayer.

In order to truly Create our Self, we must...

∞ Be Free from a false sense of security. What's the difference between false security and real security? A false security can always vanish, because it is gained through external means. Given or taken by someone or something (i.e. boss, money, etc.). Real security is born of Peace. We are defined by our experiences, only if we choose. The body may even be placed in a cell, but the mind can never be caged. In an interview with Nick Cannon, KRS One pointed out how deep this goes. "We didn't lose our land, we lost our minds. We lost our minds to go and get it. The land is still there."[149]

In order to truly Create our Self, we must...

∞ Be Free from attachment. This includes: people, places, things, thoughts, beliefs, behaviors, and so on. Even Buddha gave up his crown before receiving the Throne. We are Free to avoid altercations when we release the need to be 'right', or perceived a certain way. Someone else's perception is their business, not ours. Often the louder our reaction, the deeper the chord which was struck. Be present with its resonance, then respond. However, do so out of choice, not an assumption of correlation.

In order to truly Create our Self, we must...

∞ Be Free from fear. At the root of most fear is the illusion of death. Understand death, and we shall know **Life**. Know **Life**, and there is no death. Freedom is the ability to move without doubt. It understands that uncertainty is only a thought. Personality, the gas to its flame. Our direct connection to Truth is through the body. Allow it to move, and follow its Divine Energy. Freedom resides in our ability to remain open and vulnerable. When we stop clinging to grains of sand, and Surrender to the tides of the sea, we are Free.

Making the Most of Our Day

"We all only get 24 hours in a day. It's what we do with it that
makes a difference."

- Dr. Eric Thomas[150]

At 35 years of age, Muhammad Ali spoke with a large studio audience breaking down the time constraints of average daily living. When we consider the time spent sleeping, eating, sitting in school or an office, driving in traffic, vegging out to entertainment; how much of our Life is really dedicated to being productive?[151] We willingly give away large chunks of our day (Life), chasing things that don't really serve us. Little time, and even less Energy, is dedicated to knowing our Self. When we know our Self, all else becomes trivial. Time is currency. How we spend it is up to us. Here's what's in a 30 year checking account:

1 year = 8,544 hours

Sleeping 8 hours a day in a year = 2,920 hours (122 days sleeping. 1/3 of our year!)

1 year awake = 5,840 hours (243 days)

30 years = 256,320 hours (10,680 days)

Sleeping 8 hours a day over 30 years = 87,600 hours (3,650 days or **10 years sleeping**)

30 years awake = 175,200 hours (7,300 days or 20 years)

When people speak of following our dreams, what does that even mean? I have heard it described for the uncertain, as having the Courage to follow our curiosity. Every time we learn a skill, engage in a new behavior, or feel differently (even prior to an event); we rewrite our brain's chemistry.[152] In Life, we need not wait for 'someone' to give us a chance. Create it! The Universe will not bring us what we want, because IT feels sorry for us. We are already given all the tools necessary, to match the vibration to that which we desire. When we're truly following our dreams, we really have no choice. It moves and breathes us. Every fiber of our being is pulled in its direction.

Living our dreams requires an Honest assessment of how we spend our God given moments and Life Force Energy. Out of all the available minutes in our day, what percentage was truly spent on mastering our craft? To complain about not living our dreams, means we're not working on our dreams. There's no excuse for ignorance with a smart phone. Even taking one step towards our dream each day, creates momentum and provides a renewed sense of exuberance for Life. Maybe the first day we're jotting down ideas. By the fourth, we're looking for books that discuss these topics further, and on the seventh we're putting what we learned into action. Look how much ground we've covered towards our dream in a single week! The days begin to look different. They feel different. Everyday we're living our dream. The question is: what do we want to dream up today? Once our dreams have been infused with action, they have now become our goals. Inshallah (GOD willing), the only thing stopping us, is us.

Hard Work Leads to Flow

Kobe Bryant describes the flow state as "just being present. Now how long can you do that for?"[153] When we are functioning from the flow state, Life happens for us. Trying to categorize the moment into a predetermined set of beliefs, it happens to us. Once in the flow, the harder we work, the greater the reward. Working hard reduces risk and uncertainty. We know we're capable of greatness, because we've put in the work. We've already done it!

Accessing the flow state can occur in nearly any expression of human Life. This includes, but is not limited to: work, sex, athletics, social, and creative.[154] Functioning from the flow state (in the zone), is regarded as an experience of optimal performance, in which skill level meets the demands of a challenge, often resulting from preparation.[155] For instance, let's say I find my Self in a street fight, there is tremendous risk posed by this circumstance. However, if I know that I have practiced a cross, hook, cross and a few other hand combos to the point of muscle memory, the hard work, coaching, and dedication put in at the gym has significantly reduced my risk and uncertainty. As Bruce Lee said, "I fear not the man who has practiced 10,000 kicks once, but I fear the man that has practiced one kick 10,000 times."[156]

Other factors associated with functioning from the flow state include, but are not limited to: definable goals; immediate performance feedback; a feeling of control; time transformation; a loss of self-consciousness; immersion of action and awareness; subjective intrinsic value in the experience; cognitive flexibility; and a high degree of concentration.[157] All of which are outcomes of a deep meditative

146

practice/experience.[158] Research indicates that both flow state and mindfulness involve living in the present moment, Free from worry. In fact, they are so similar, it has been suggested that they may simply be variant stages on a continuum.[159]

Every moment offers its own celebration. Every struggle an opportunity for growth. Feeling that we can fail at anything is a great illusion. Flow with Life, and let the moment guide our movement. If we fail, it is because we are living for tomorrow. It's like surfing a wave and thinking about the next one we're going to catch. WHILE WE'RE RIDING THIS WAVE!

One Chance at this Life

"We can fail at what we don't want to do in Life. So we might as well take a chance and do what we Love."

- Jim Carrey[160]

We forfeit our Peace when we forego pursuing and living our dreams. This book is presented in hopes that we will begin to cherish our moments more. To remind us to stop selling our Self short, and make the most of GOD's blessings. Peace is always within us. Wherever we go, and whatever we do, IT IS ALWAYS HERE AND NOW. Infinity is found in a moment, and we are not separate from THIS MOMENT. Every fiber of existence serves a purpose. Even the pyramids are composed of grains of sand. It is amazing what can be built with vision, focus, and collaboration. Our lives are ours to build. GOD is the Architect, we are the Carpenters. Every option of design has already been created. Some are Taj Mahals, others cozy bungalows tucked away on a beautiful island with all our family and friends. Which do we choose to tune to? Which are we choosing to live out right now?

Significant Insignificance

Hospice patients often report that their biggest regret was not living a Life true to themselves.[161] There are approximately 250 billion stars in our galaxy. Just our galaxy! Each star (sun) in each galaxy is estimated to have an average of 1.6 planets in its solar system. The observable universe is estimated to contain two-hundred billion to two trillion galaxies. In this universe of great possibilities, how can we do anything but live our dreams? Our Life is an expression of significant insignificance. Life goes on, whether we're here or not. Why not make the most of it?

Look into the eyes of another and we shall find an entire universe. A Universe is contained within each of us. The neurons in brain cells (*left image*) look just like the macro Universe (*right image*) when examined through a high powered microscope.

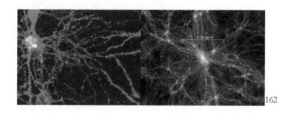

162

A little investigation and we will find this goes well beyond the excuse of pareidolia (the phenomenon of perceiving and/or attaching human characteristics or patterns to inanimate or neutral stimuli). From the micro to the macro, we are reflections and extensions of GOD. Endowed with the Power to Co-Create our Life through perception and choice. Right now we can choose Love, Peace, Health, Strength and Happiness. Compassion and Understanding. Freedom and Appreciation. This very moment, we can choose to live our Life as an expression of Divinity. The choice is ours, and breath our compass.

~ One LOVE. One GOD

Questions:

1. What does my Heaven on Earth look like?

    _____

    _____

    _____

2. What does it feel like?

    _____

    _____

    _____

Additional Notes:

_____

_____

_____

_____

_____

_____

_____

APPENDIX

VARIOUS BREATHING MEDITATIONS

"Breathing and Feeling are synonymous."

- Shantam Nityama[163]

I f we knew that this was going to be our last breath in this body, would we enjoy it? We average about 16 breaths a minute, 960 an hour, and well over 22K breaths per day.[164] How many of these breaths are Conscious? How we breathe, is how we live. What is our breathing telling us right now?

According to Osho, every individual has a pattern and rhythm to their breathing as unique as a thumbprint.[165] Therefore, to teach breathing, is false. One simply needs to enter a state of Witnessing to become Aware of the breath. The duration of our inhalations and exhalations alters with each emotion. Where is our breath located? Our nose, chest, or navel? Continuously watching our breath reveals that we are not even the ones breathing, we are being breathed. Breath is without face. The subject soon fades, ultimately revealing, that only breathing exists.

Connecting with our breath is an excellent method to open the door to the here and now. It can further be used to enhance our sex Life.[166] In Hindu culture, breath is regarded as prana, which means Life. Breath is Life, and Life is LOVE. This section will explore several techniques to connect deeper with our breath.

At This Moment

Just today, breathe and enjoy each moment. Each breath. Tomorrow will come and we can worry if we need to then. The past isn't going anywhere either. We can concern ourselves about that tomorrow as well. Today, breathe. Breathe fully. Breathe Consciously. We may forget and wander down familiar roads. All good. We can still breathe there too. Breathe. Witness. Enjoy.

The first technique is learning how to move our Awareness.

Here is an easy way to get acquainted:

∞ First hold out your hand, and place all of your presence on the very tip of your right index finger. All of your presence, all of your Awareness is centered at the tip of your right index finger. Feel the heart beat pulsating through the tip of the finger.

∞ Take as long as is needed. Be still and feel this.

∞ This same Awareness/presence, will be used to follow our breath. Once we have the experience of connecting with this

Awareness, we will find it useful in all other meditation techniques.

As a side note, while engaging in any meditation technique, a feeling of fear may arise. A deep anxiety that *Oh shit! I'm going to die.* Be present with this as well. Allow this to be. Melt into this. Fighting or running from it will only make it worse. It is True, a part of us is dying. However, that which dies, can never truly live. As this fear fades, we melt into The Oneness. Again, I find it beneficial to set an alarm when meditating. This allows us to melt into the moment, without worrying if five minutes is up yet?

Buddha Breath[167]

Use our Awareness to follow the breath throughout the entirety of its cycle. In through the nose, down the esophagus, chest cavity, and into the stomach. Let the stomach and belly button rise up with air. There's a space. Follow the breath up the exact same path through the body and out the nose. Now there's another space. Be Aware of the space between both breaths (inhalation and exhalation). That's where we truly exist. This will provide a glimpse into the space from which thoughts (and feelings) arise.

Fire Breath

This involves short, Powerful, rapid breathing through the nostrils (some practices even encourage alternate nostril breathing with this technique). The duration of the breath can be adjusted for different affects upon the body/mind. Here, the breath is forced into

153

(inhalation), and out of the nose (exhalation), very quickly without break. Make sure we are sitting or lying down when we first begin this technique to avoid falling over. We can begin with 50 quick breaths, and then build from there. Be present throughout the entire breath. At the completion of the cycle, Witness the Silence. The purpose of the fire and warrior breath (described next) is to flood the body with oxygen. This further serves as an excellent method to release emotional trauma from the body. Performing a couple of sets of this technique can quickly quiet the mind.

Warrior Breath

This breathing technique is very similar to the fire breath. The only difference is that the focus is placed solely on the inhalation. Allow the exhalation to happen of its own accord. Air will escape, that's fine. However, do not force it. Remember, the difference during the fire breath is that the air is forced both in and out of the nostrils.

Spinal and Organ Breathing

Focusing our Awareness, as described in the Buddha breath meditation, demonstrates that we can breathe with any area of our body. Spinal breathing is a Powerful, Strengthening exercise. It is recommended to begin slow. We can also utilize our breath to increase the vitality of our organs (which as described in the chapter on Consciousness, are alive and associated with various emotions). For this practice, the five main organs are: kidneys, liver, lungs, spleen, and heart. Each of us will be drawn to focus on specific organs a little more than others. Make sure to avoid neglecting the remaining four, as doing so may cause further imbalances.

Hyperventilation

This technique was shared and developed by Wim Hof. He reports to have been greatly influenced by Tibetan monks practicing Tummo meditation.[168] The purpose is to flood the body with oxygen, again bringing us to a state of Witnessing. Wim Hof suggests that the body takes in only a fraction of necessary and available oxygen, due to a lack of proper breathing throughout the day.[169] Utilizing this technique, when coupled with cold immersion (to be discussed later in this section on meditation), individuals have demonstrated an ability to access and influence the autonomous nervous system.[170] Science previously believed this to be a physiologically impossible feat. Wim Hof, as well as individuals he has trained in this technique, have been studied in the science lab.

For instance, a group of 12 healthy, males were injected with a bacterial endotoxin known to cause severe flu-like symptoms. The intervention group was instructed in the Wim Hof Method (WHM) [meditation, breathing techniques, and exposure to cold] for 10 days prior. The adrenaline produced on command by the trained group (sitting in a hospital bed, hooked up to monitoring equipment) registered higher than an individual bungee jumping. This resulted in the trained group demonstrating a greater ability to fight off the symptoms of the bacterial endotoxin, such as fever and flu-like symptoms, than that of the control group.[171]

To perform this technique, same with the fire or warrior breath, make sure to be sitting or lying down to avoid falling and hurting oneself. This breath is very similar to the warrior breath, except oxygen is taken in through the mouth. However, the principle remains the same. Suck in as much oxygen as possible all the way down into the stomach. Imagine the stomach is like a balloon that we are blowing up.[172] Now, here I have seen the exhale explained two different ways. We will cover the one I have more experience with. This technique recommends to not purposefully breathe out. If some oxygen escapes, that is fine. Bring in as much oxygen as possible with each breath. The purpose is to maintain as much oxygen in the body as we can. Perform thirty to forty of these breaths. Keep a timer nearby, or better yet, just feel into it. As soon as the last breath is taken in, hold the breath in the body. Remain as long as possible without exhaling or inhaling any more oxygen (don't push so far as to cause harm). When nearing the point of being unable to hold the breath any longer, draw in one more large breath all the way down into the stomach. Continue holding the breath for another fifteen seconds. Release the breath, and allow the body to return to its normal state of breathing. Witness this breath, this Silence. Perform this for two or three sets if desired. We will likely be able to hold the breath even longer next time. A noticeable and immediate difference in the function, Health, and vitality of the body/mind will be felt. This exercise further serves to highlight how little air we are actually taking in throughout the day. If we were at full capacity, we would be unable to perform such a feat, as our lungs and cells could not allow any more air in.

Paced Breathing

Here we can vary the rhythm of our inhalation and/or exhalation for a chosen amount of time. For instance, breathe in for a count of five seconds, and then exhale for a count of five seconds. Sticking with this time frame, another approach is to breathe in for five seconds, exhale for five seconds, then do not inhale or exhale for five seconds. Continuing this practice for a desired amount of time or repetitions. The timing of either technique can vary based on comfort, experience, and desired outcome.

Alternate Nostril Breathing

This method simply practices paced breathing through one nostril. Plugging the other nostril by pressing on the outside of our nose. Once the desired repetitions are complete, switch nostrils. This will help to correct imbalances in our breathing, and therefore our body.

WITNESSING MEDITATIONS

Observational Breathing Meditation[173]

T his has been included as a Witnessing meditation, as it is not a manipulation of breath. Rather, a simple observation. This is an excellent method to connect with our Original Breath. Osho suggests to Witness the breath throughout our daily activities. Monitor the inhalation and exhalation, unattached to either. The duration of each will change with our emotions. For example, when feeling pleasure, notice if the inhale is longer than the exhale. Does this alter as intensity increases? We can observe the breath throughout any emotion. We may even keep a weekly chart assessing our breathing, and examining the data for themes. Did any emotions occur more than others last week? What was going on, and was this a benefit or detriment in our Life?

For instance:

Emotion	Inhalation	Exhalation
i.e. Joy	(duration)	(duration)

Life is a Drama Meditation

See the world (and Life) as a play in a Cosmic theatre. Have fun with it, but do not be attached. For example, if anger arises, ask, "Who is experiencing this anger?" "Where is this anger?" So often we identify our Self with our thoughts, emotions, and behaviors. We have been conditioned to forget that this is not who we are. It's like a mighty river identifying itself with one stagnant pool of water a couple klicks upstream. This technique works well with any thought, feeling, or behavior. Vitvan has advised that we **must condition our Self to Witness everything in existence as a configuration of units of Energy.**[174] This includes thoughts, feelings, objects, and so on.

This is much easier during times of Joy. It becomes a whole other practice while in the midst of conflict, anger, sadness, anxiety, lust, et cetera. All provide a wonderful opportunity to ask our Self, "who is feeling this" or "where does this have roots"? This meditation provides a tool to remain Peaceful in any situation. Moving deeper into our natural state of Witnessing. Pure, untouched, and unaffected by the milieu of influence.

KRS One Witness Meditation[175]

This meditation practice is extremely helpful in realizing the Witness. This provides insight and access to an entirely new range of Awareness that has always been present. Try this. Look for something to read. It can be anything. A nutrition label, the title of a nearby book, a receipt, whatever. Obviously you're reading this book, so even try it with the cover if you like. Just make sure whatever is read, is a short phrase at most. Now, on the count of three, read the word, but do not speak it out loud. Ready? One. Two. Three. "_____".

You heard what was read, right? Now, how is this possible? When we speak a word out loud, this creates sound vibrations that ricochet off of objects in the environment, which are reflected back to our ears.

The vibration then travels from our ears and into the brain. The brain registers and deciphers the vibratory frequency, and it is then translated into an audible sound. These sounds are often associated with symbols (a word or a combination of words).

A similar process occurs through sight. The image first registers in the brain as a vibratory frequency before being translated. However, say we are told to imagine a pink turtle. We can close our eyes, and right before us is a pink turtle (after strengthening this muscle, we need not even close our eyes). So who is hearing, and who is seeing this internal phenomenon? That which is beyond ego. The Witness. Again, ultimately there is no Witness, just Witnessing. Even feeling this once and we are forever changed. KRS One regards this as entering the fifth dimension.

Feel the Space from Which Thoughts Arise

As we realize our inner, ever present Silence; we grow accustomed to Witnessing the river of thoughts flowing through us. As mentioned in the Buddha Breath, eventually we reach an Awareness of the space from which thoughts arise. Just a glimpse, and it is always available. We are then able to tap into this space upon command. At first this may appear as the space between breaths (when doing the Buddha Breath meditation), later, these gaps will grow in duration and consistency. These gaps reveal the ocean behind the rhythm of its waves. As Shantam Nityama has enlightened, "this Silence is our very nature. That's all that exists. Unless we buy into all the lies that were fed to us."

Emptiness Meditation

Emptiness will reveal the fullness of Life. We are everything and nothing all at the same time. Mindfulness techniques are used to arrive at a state of Emptiness.[176] As Bruce Lee has said, "empty your mind. Be formless, shapeless."[177] A study examining differences between mindfulness, and 'emptiness' meditation, found that individuals practicing 'emptiness' meditation reported greater improvements in the following outcomes: nonattachment, mystical experiences, and psycho-spiritual well-being.[178] Emptiness meditation can be boiled down to the following:

1. Enter a state of Witnessing.

2. Understand that any stimulus surfacing (thought, feeling, experience, et cetera) is not who we Truly Are.

3. Osho suggests it is as simple as stating, "not this." Then continue Witnessing the Emptiness of our being.

4. We are the Void. The Source from which all arises and returns.

SILENCE MEDITATION

Meditation increases our Awareness of the ever present Silence within us. This goes well beyond Witnessing the chattering mind. Silence speaks all languages, and is the Space from which all existence blossoms. There are several steps we can take to cultivate this Silence in our daily Life. Let's first examine our external environment before addressing our internal one.

The Feng Shui of External Noise

What does our home space look like? How does it feel? What is the sound of this space? Although Harmony ultimately exists even in chaos, a cluttered or dirty living space is reflective of an internal discord in need of cleaning. All change begins within. Sometimes these wounds or issues do not show themselves so readily. When constantly distracted or engaged in outside events, they are easily overlooked. Hence, the appeal of diverting our attention to the affairs of the trite and mundane. Oftentimes, that which is outside our control.

It is our choice how we keep our home. Whether it be a mansion, apartment, tin shack with a dirt yard, or even a vehicle; we always possess the ability to keep our surrounding area clean. If blessed to have a home, begin the day by making the bed. As Tim Ferris says, we have now accomplished our first task for the day.[179] When we retire for the evening, we will return to a clean and organized bed.

We not only ingest food into our body, but also the entirety of our environment (sights, sounds, smells, et cetera). This stimuli is then

162

ingrained into every cell of our being. We must therefore choose carefully. Paying close attention to the vibrational effect of the music we listen to, entertainment we watch, and speech in which we engage.

It is important to also shut off from the "white noise" of daily Life. White noise is regarded as background noise. For instance, the television at the gym running a program (wow, revelations revealed through words). The effects of white noise are not only damaging to our psyche, but also to our physiology. This goes for wildlife as well. For example, although difficult to measure, a meta-analysis of two decades worth of scientific research indicates that increased noise has had the following negative effects on wildlife: altered vocal behavior, reduced abundance, changes in vigilance and foraging, diminished physical fitness, and an altered structure in ecological communities.[180] There is a reason militaries use sound to torture prisoners, control behavior, and disable the 'enemy'.

Moving with Silence

Taking time to sit in Silence is healing for the Soul. This provides a frame of reference for when moving through daily activities. Once functioning from our internal Silence, we are hypervigilant as to what we choose to allow into our field of Consciousness. That which disturbs our Peace, no longer has a place in our Life.

Spending a Day in Silence

Moving in Silence will heighten our sensory awareness. We will find a well of Energy that had been covered in debris and distracted into dormancy. When engaged in this meditation technique, we are often reminded of that phone call we have to make, the email that needs our attention, that text that must be returned, the neighbor who is hungry or lonely, and so on. Sometimes these are legitimate concerns, but take careful examination of when we are using 'others' as an excuse to avoid our own discomfort with our Self-imposed Silence.

This doesn't entail acting like a pompous jack ass to everyone who talks with us during our vow of Silence. For example, say we're grabbing a cup of tea and the barista at the café asks how's our day. A simple, "Life is good. Thanks. How about your Self?" may brighten her day. When not worried about what we're going to say next, watch how much more we listen to, and feel, her response. Feel the difference in how we speak and what we prioritize as worthy content to share. For those who absolutely do not want to break their Silence, I have seen people carry around a note politely informing others of their chosen Silence. Even this serves to put a smile on someone's face.

How to Listen

Words are a poor substitute for communication…

Effective listening skills have been associated with better overall communication and persuasive skills.[181] In the 1999 film, Fight Club, Edward Norton's character (who remained nameless) was speaking with Marla Singer. She asked why he attended terminal illness support

164

groups when he was completely healthy. He replied, "I don't know. It's like, when people think that you're dying, they're really interested in what you have to say. Instead of…" Marla interrupted, "Instead of just waiting for their turn to speak?!" "Yea" he replied as his voice lowered, depressed he was unable to complete his thought.

A dialogue is defined as a conversation between two or more people.[182] How much of this interaction is truly organic? We can read books and study videos on how to 'talk with anyone', however, an authentic conversation is the result of listening. Listening is Openness. It is a complete Surrender to the moment. It is allowing our Self to flow downstream without agenda. Uncertain of our destination, but centered each step of the way.

So much of communication today is one-sided. The culture of the last decade has reduced face to face conversations to snippets and cliff notes. The beauty and blessings of this century's technological advancements, require a greater diligence in ensuring that heart to heart communication still occurs. Much of Life is now executable from a bubble. Homes, vehicles, and jobs encapsulate worldviews. Later, confined to the orbit of our phones after our shift. Walking the streets with our heads down, and oblivious to the 'outside' world. Not only the dangers of the terrain, but also the beauty accompanying each step. Consciously listening to our internal and external environment, opens us to the symphony of Life.

A Practice

This meditation was influenced by Osho (the Book of Secrets) and Hazrat Inyat Khan (The Mysticism of Sound and Music). When engaged in daily activity, allow the sounds of the moment, and all that exists within this moment, to penetrate one's being. Listen without intellectualizing. We need not attach words to anything. For instance, birds chirping. Don't listen to the pitched rhythms and tones then allocate them to the 'chirps' of a 'bird'. Just listen. Allow them to flow freely throughout all existence, including us.

This does not mean that we become a sounding board for people venting. There are plenty of people who will take advantage of an open heart and available ear. That's on them, and when you spot them, if it's addressed and they persist, do what's best for Self. We owe them absolutely nothing. Respect and Understanding have nothing to do with wasting our Life Force on those attempting to syphon it. Pushing us to co-sign to whatever delusion of self-grandeur they may have authored.

Music is found in every movement. The chirping of birds, flight of a jet, or a neighbor's laughter all have an immediate affect on the vibration of our being, and the rhythm of our breath. Paying attention to this correlation in our daily lives, we are better able to sort and choose what we give attention to. Our vibration, mood, and ultimately our day; are the result of what we choose to **focus** on.

COLD IMMERSION MEDITATION

Wim Hof has popularized cold immersion, and is renowned for his feats of Strength and endurance with the cold. Check his website to learn more about the Wim Hof Method and available trainings.[183] Exposure to the cold, such as a shower or ice bath, not only serves as an excellent meditation technique to enter the state of Witnessing; it also provides many health benefits. [184] This includes, but is not limited to: increased alertness; refined hair and skin; strengthened immune system; improved blood circulation; weight loss; stress relief; antidepressant properties; increased fertility in men; and a reduction in muscle soreness and expedited recovery times after exercise.[185]

This technique can be adapted to a variety of cold environments. However, if entering a cold body of water, such as a glacier lake, it is not always advisable to lower oneself below the neck. Nor, to enter a depth or distance that would be difficult to return to shore, if the body locked up. One of the Health benefits of cold immersion is that the blood leaves the extremities (those parts of the body which are not one hundred percent mandatory for immediate survival) and moves into the vital organs. Bringing with it potent doses of oxygen, plasma, vitamins, nutrients, and electrolytes. When not in an environment necessitating immediate survival, like being stuck on the top of Everest, blood will circulate and return to the limbs once removed from the cold.

Warming Up to the Idea of a Cold Shower

If not comfortable jumping right in, start with a hot shower, and then finish with a minute or two in the cold. Get the water as cold as tolerable, while continuing to push and break barriers of what was previously believed possible. When it first touches the body, it may sting or feel like pins and needles all over. We may even begin hyperventilating. Connect with the breath, while Witnessing the sensations of the body. For example, if the arm feels cold, allow it to feel cold. Feel its intensity. Watch this feeling as if it were happening to someone else. This exercise will further drive home the realization that these bodies are rentals. Vehicles for our Consciousness to experience Life.

While Cold Understand...

I am not cold, for there is no 'I'. There is just cold. Melt into this 'coldness'. Witness it in its entirety. This is how the Divine is choosing to express Itself in this moment.

MELTING INTO THE MOMENT MEDITATION

Feel the Universe converging into us. Taken even further, Osho suggests to feel the Cosmos flow through us.[186] For instance, sun rays touch our skin and travel right through, never breaking stride. The wind fills our vessel, touching every fiber of our being as it hums unencumbered on its path. This can be done with anything. Sights, sounds, Light, it makes no difference. So often in conversation, our words bounce off of one another. The ego serves as a forcefield. We look like Superman deflecting bullets. The content of conversation stands little chance of registering in the heart. Allow the sounds of sentences, words, music, et cetera to pass through the empty halls of our being. We are unaffected, yet forever changed.

MELTING INTO THE LIGHT MEDITATION

We are beacons of Light. Everything in Existence is Light. When sitting, allow this Light to flow down and into the top of our head, through our body and into our root. Allow thoughts, feelings, experiences, attachments, and all which no longer serves us, to melt into the brilliance of this white Light. Feel its warmth. Breathe this Light in and out of our body. Allow this Light to flow outward into the world, emanating from every fiber of our being. Now allow our body to melt into this Light. Existing only as a breathing Light. Rejoin the body. Breathe Light into the body a little while longer. Bring this Light into the world.

GRATITUDE MEDITATION

G ratitude is within. As Gratitude evolves to Appreciation, we will discover even more to be Grateful for. Expressing Gratefulness even for the miniscule, we are giving Praise to God. Whether we are having sex or taking a shit, we can still give Thanks to God. I offer these examples, not to offend, but to give a glimpse into the breadth of all that we have to be Thankful for. We can connect with this feeling at our discretion.

For this meditation:

1. Focus on your greatest, most Joyful, Loving experience that you can recall right now.

2. Connect with this feeling.

3. Breathe this feeling.

4. Continue breathing this feeling.

5. Move, live, and enjoy. It's that easy.

Gratitude is Alchemy for the Soul

Even that which flat out sucks may offer something to Appreciate. For instance, depression, pain, anxiety, or injury. It's amazing how quickly things turn around with this practice. And it is a practice. One moment at a time. That's the beautiful thing about Life, it's never too late to live. Eventually, we'll strengthen this muscle to the point of instinct.

A Sample Prayer:

Thank You God for blessing this and all Life with your Holiest of Holies. Thank you Holy Divine Mother, Holy Divine Father, Ancestors, Guides, and Protecting Spirits for Guiding me towards my Highest Self. Thank you for the breath in this body, and thank you for this body. Thank you for blessing all Life, and opening all doors to that which is good and a blessing, and closing all doors to that which wishes to do harm. Thank you for blessing all Life, across all time, space, and dimensions with: LOVE, Light, Life, Peace, Creativity, Freedom, Health, Wealth, Wisdom, and Power. Thank you for blessing all Life with Patience, Faith, Understanding, Guidance, Protection, Joy, and Harmony. Thank you for Strength, Courage, Mercy and Forgiveness. Thank You GOD for all that is, was, and ever will be.

FEELING MEDITATION

Tuning into the Body

"The Body never lies."

-Shantam Nityama[187]

Everyday tasks have a tendency to become mundane, overlooked, and rushed through. This is an exercise to bring us back to our bodies. Centering our Awareness in the navel will reveal the Peace/Silence which is always within us. Once we're present in our bodies, it's much easier to use this body (our inner Guidance System) as a tuning fork to become aware of our Truth. We can then confidently ask our Self:

"How am I feeling right now?"

"Am I even feeling right now?"

These questions invoke presence and Truth in our daily lives. When checking in, if the answer comes back, "I'm not." That's a Powerful reminder to immediately shift our **focus**. Connect with the body, then move. Remember, it is a Divine vehicle for our Consciousness to navigate this plane. We can connect with any part of our body, by moving our Awareness to this location. If feeling unable to connect, physically touch a body part, any body part. The heart, or even a finger for example. Feel the heartbeat in wherever was touched. Stay with this feeling for a moment. Breathe into it. Revisit the section on breathing meditations (in the Appendix) to understand how to move Awareness through our body.

QI GONG (MOVEMENT MEDITATION)

"50 trillion cells. Each cell has about 1.4 volts of electricity. Every cell has a cell positive voltage (proton) inside a cell negative voltage (neuron/neutron). Every cell is a live battery. The human body then can produce 700 trillion volts of electricity!!"

- Dr. Bruce Lipton[188]

Qi Gong is regarded as a movement meditation. Energy flows throughout all existence, including us. We are made of Energy. Breath and Energy are intimately related. Through practice Truth is revealed. Qi Gong is regarded as a practical and effective healing modality.[189] Practitioners of Qi Gong demonstrate increased Peace, Power, Strength, endurance, and flexibility throughout their lives.

In Practice:

1. Eckart Toelle suggests sitting Silently and feel the Energy coming out of our hands.[190]

2. We can also rub our hands together to bring greater sensation and Awareness into the hands.

3. To connect and feel this, place hands in front of the body.

4. Move hands close together without touching. Move them further apart while remaining present with the feeling surrounding, and in-between the hands.

5. Play with this, moving the hands closer together and further apart. Continue not to touch the hands together.

Eventually, we will become Aware of the Energy flowing between our hands. The Energy between our hands has been compared to feeling magnets.[191] For me, when it first hit, I felt like I was holding an invisible water balloon. Again, this Energy is Omnipresent and everywhere. We have now only focused our attention on IT. We can now guide the Energy anywhere. Love, Creativity, Respect, and responsibility are mandatory.

SEXUAL PLEASURE MEDITATIONS

"What happens with your sex energy depends on how you use it. What it can become does not depend on it alone, but on your understanding, and on how you live your Life."

- Osho[192]

We are whole unto our Self. Once we have connected with the LOVE within, the LOVE that sustains and breathes all of existence, we are ready and able to connect with 'others'. The term 'making Love' is quite misleading. It gives the impression that we must do something to our partner. That we must perform in a certain manner, or memorize a sequence of awe inspiring techniques to bring the other to a state of orgasmic bliss. As Osho and Nityama have discussed, orgasmicness is our very nature. This Divine Energy seeks a natural expression through our bodies. It becomes blocked, depleted, or stagnated through painful thought patterns or Life experiences.

Nityama has guided that being orgasmic, is really just being comfortable enough with our Self, and/or our partner, to breathe.[193] The Energy will take over from there. Sometimes this shows up as a light touch and a barely audible exhale. Other moments, IT may find expression through screams that resonate unbridled pleasure in the spines of neighbors three blocks down the road. Just as with any expedition into space, making Love is to be an exploration, not a conquest. Allowing the 'other' to express themselves fully, our

177

presence and Appreciation are the greatest gifts we can offer our Lover. The moment will guide the movement, the depth of our Surrender will temper its expansion.

Many people believe there's nothing left to learn about pleasure and sex. Remaining closed-mind and captured to advertisement's whims. "It's a biological phenomenon! Primates aren't taught how to bang." They're also not building spaceships, or creating works of art that will inspire future generations. Thinking we know the answer, before we even hear the question, is like watching two seconds of a movie and convinced we know the whole plot (although some Hollywood productions may warrant such expedience).

*I realize that the following language and topics may make some people uncomfortable. However, in order to effectively communicate the breadth of these practices, it is necessary. The reader is advised to proceed at their discretion for the remainder of this book.

Orgasmic Breathing

My study and practice of the Energy Bodywork has taught me that much trauma is stored in our genitals. Therefore, if we do not address this, we will fail to get to the root of the issue negatively affecting our Life. It will continue showing up as anger, fear, jealousy, insecurity, and so on in our relationships. Releasing this trauma, our eyes open to a whole new world. Again, if the following language/subject matter makes the reader uneasy, then now may be a good place to stop. However, remember, it is just us reading this. There is no one looking over our shoulder. Also, if urged to skip, it may be beneficial to ask ourselves "why?" first. As has been taught to me, in order to grow, we have to learn to be comfortable in our uncomfortableness.[194]

Focusing our Awareness on our genitals, breathe with the genitals. This may involve fast breathing techniques such as the fire or warrior breath, or deep, slow breathing into and around the genitals. Women can also breathe from their breasts. Make sure to breathe from both breasts, centering Awareness on the nipples. Genital breathing will serve to enhance our sexual sensitivity and release physical and emotional traumas. Traumas stored throughout the body, including the genitals, and can serve to block or inhibit the flow of Energy through our natural channels. Over time, these can be physically felt. They will appear in the breasts and genitals like tiny grains of rice. At this point, they need to be massaged out of the body. When doing so, this may trigger a memory of the event that caused the pain. If you feel like crying, allow it. The burden is no longer yours to carry.

If they remain, the body eventually shuts down and no longer registers the constant pleasure flowing through it. As the blockages are removed, we increase the amount of Energy (Chi, also spelt Qi or Ki) that is now accessible to us. Greater sensitivity, means greater Awareness of our natural state, which is Orgasmic.[195] This will serve to enhance all aspects of our Life, including making Love.

When the Polarities Meet

Men, be present in your penis, testicles, and prostate. Women, be present in your breasts. In Tantra and Taoism, these are regarded as each gender's positive poles. The negative (receptive) poles to the circuit are as follows: men/chest, women/vagina. Positive penetrates negative. Negative receives positive. Positive is electric by nature, negative is magnetic. This is beyond our concepts of 'good' and 'bad'. 'Positive' and 'negative' are still two sides to the same coin, two expressions of the same Energy. Sex is constantly taking place. Even in conversation. Speaking and listening (penetrating and receiving). Insertion is a mechanical substitute for real sex. When a woman has been entered by a man, his positive pole is charging her negative pole (receptive). A woman enters the man through the heart. Her positive pole is charging his negative pole (receptive). When truly open, each will feel the Love and Power flowing from, and into one another. This finds infinite form through the Formless. While making Love, the poles may even flicker and briefly switch between partners, regardless of gender.

Pleasure Through Sonar

Each voice is a unique instrument of the Soul. To be Free, we must allow our sounds. For example, when making Love, allowing our sounds their natural expression is healing. Inspiring greater pleasure. There is no need to be scared of being heard. As Nityama says, our sounds of ecstasy are the greatest gift we can ever give our Partner. The voice is a compass. Otherwise, we're basically searching for each other in the dark.[196] A cross cultural study found that people who were born deaf, laughed and sneezed differently from people who hear and therefore associate words such as 'achoo', or 'haha' with the action.[197] Sounds still occurred, however, pitches and tones varied significantly. That's pretty incredible. Language has even infiltrated our laughter and sneezing. In what other ways have we been conditioned to stifle our authenticity?

180

Why are we comfortable going berserk at a sporting event, yet guilt-ridden and ashamed to let out more than a peep when engaging in the very thing that brings Life to this planet?! Pleasure is an infinite well for Joy and healing. Moaning, laughing, crying, screaming, and/or anything in between are all essential expressions of the human Spirit. Sometimes it's perfectly natural for this full spectrum to appear in a single Love making session.

Practice to have No-Technique

Teacher: "I see your talents have gone beyond the mere physical level. Your skills are now at the point of spiritual insight. I have several questions. What is the highest technique you hope to achieve?"

Bruce Lee: "To have no technique."[198]

That being said, techniques can still serve to enhance the Lover prior to enjoinment with a partner. Again, we have no business connecting with 'another' until we have connected with our Self. Know, and be willing to explore what makes us feel good regularly. Many religious and public educational systems regard this practice as masturbation. The seeking of pleasure through bodily senses until orgasm is 'achieved'. We have been conditioned to forget that every touch, breath, and moment is orgasmic. We just have to melt into IT. I prefer the term Self-pleasure. Approaching our Self with revere, curiosity, and understanding. Not seeking to just 'get one off'. Which is how a large portion of us have been conditioned to engage in sex.

The Rhythm of the Moment

Allow the expression of the moment to guide the movement. As Bruce Lee once said, "if you enter a fight with the intention to bite, that's a good way to lose your teeth. However, when used at the right time, it may very well save your Life."[199] The same could be said of making Love. A nibble on a shoulder or the back of a neck may sometimes be just what the doctor ordered. Research into the Kama Sutra will reveal that various positions stimulate the body in different ways. Each offering a varying degree of intensity and pleasure. The imagination is our only limit. In Taoism, it is taught for a man to enter a woman by alternating between rhythms of deep and shallow thrusts. To incorporate more circular motions, rather than functioning solely as a mechanical piston.

When making Love, let the moment provide the melody, while the breath serves as its metronome. Allow breathing. The moment we stop our breath, we shut ourselves off from Life. Prior to connecting with a Partner, it's important to Understand our Self.

Self-Pleasure

When Self-pleasuring, take time. There is no rush. There is no goal to be reached. Let each moment be a celebration of the Divine. If one suffers insecurity resulting from body dysmorphia (or a distorted or negative body image), it may be beneficial to get comfortable self-pleasuring in front of a mirror for a little while. Learning to Love our Self as we are. However, a prolonged practice in front of the mirror, say for years on end, or every time we self-pleasure; could be just as detrimental as enduring a negative body image. It creates an attachment to imagery, which is of the mind. Rather than feeling, breathing, and being fully present in this moment.

Pleasuring for the sake of release is masturbation. Done consistently over a long period of time is draining and harmful to our well-being. This is why even after one bust, people often go to sleep. It is the body's way of shutting down all unnecessary functions and going into recovery mode. Basically, making sure the organs are not taxed with any unnecessary tasks while the body refuels.

A Practice:

1. Make some time for Self. Even if it is just in the shower, connect with Self.

2. We can incorporate organic oil(s), such as unprocessed, virgin coconut oil.

3. Begin by lightly touching the positive poles slowly.

4. Pay special attention to the breath.

5. Allow the body to move naturally. If the pelvis wants to move, let it. Allow the orgasmic wave to flow through the whole body. We will eventually find our Self submerged in One Orgasmic Ocean.

6. Allow our authentic sounds to be released (aim for privacy, but if the household does not allow for that, then muffle the sounds into a towel).

7. Circulate the Energy through the Cosmic Orbit.

The Cosmic Orbit

When Self-pleasuring (or making Love with a partner) allow the sexual Energy (Life Force Energy) to flow through its natural channels. First, by breathing and Surrendering into the moment. Self-pleasure is invigorating and revitalizing. This is accomplished by circulating the Energy. In the Taoist practice, this is regarded as the Cosmic Orbit (for both genders). Further information can be found by studying the vast amount of work produced by Mantak Chia.

In essence, Consciously direct this Energy from our genitals and up our spine. Allow the Energy to rise up the spine, and circulate it through the top of the head, then down into the third eye. In the Taoist practice, this is one meridian (Energy channel). Touching the tip of the tongue to the roof of our mouth, we connect the circuit with the second meridian. Allow the Energy to flow down the front of our body. It will circulate down through the throat, chest, stomach, navel, sacral, and back into the genitals.

This is the largest, but only one of many, Energy circuits in our body. This is a natural path for our sexual Energy. As mentioned, Life experiences dam up its flow. Once these blockages are removed, our Life is back on course.

Orgasm and Ejaculation Are Not Synonymous

The Cosmic Orbit may also be used to forego ejaculation in both sexes. In fact, greater orgasmicness will be realized through this practice. When arriving close to the point of ejaculation, cease movement, and breathe the Energy up through the Cosmic Orbit.

When control of the seed is regained, begin again. I have found melting (Surrendering) into this Energy brings one into a deeper state of relaxation and Witnessing. Allow the Energy to flow with Divine order. Outside the interference of ego and its desires. When becoming Aware of blockages, breathe this orgasmic Energy into that part of the body. Moving deeper, breathe the Energy as that body part. For example, if the kidneys are harboring fear, breathe the kidneys. Again, there are several other 'techniques' that can be learned and practiced, and it is highly recommended to look into the work of Mantak Chia and Shophar Graves for greater insights.

A Special Note for the Masculine

It should be mentioned, there is nothing 'wrong' with ejaculation whatsoever. If it happens and it wasn't desired, it's just an opportunity to strengthen one's practice. Not beat ourselves up over it. That's an integral part as to how our species reproduces, expands, and evolves. However, spacing out one's releases will provide greater vigor and Life satisfaction to all those involved. We will gain access to greater Creativity, as well as an enhanced intuition, Strength, and cognitive function. As a Lover, it is vital to remain in control of one's seed. Not become overwhelmed by the pleasure of our partner. If feeling out of 'control' and on the verge of release, this is often a reflection that we simply are not breathing. Connect with the breath, and if needed, slow down and **focus** on the exhale. This will calm the sea, as we are then able to remain fully present with our Partner. Treat every wave like the ride of your Life (in and out of the bedroom). Our capacity for pleasure is Infinite.

BIBLIOGRAPHY

1 Naimy, M. (1988). *The Book of Mirdad.* Watkins Publishing.

2 KRS One. (2009). *The Gospel of Hip Hop: The first instrument.* Powerhouse.

3 Krian Music Group. (2013, February 6). Dead Prez "no way as the way" official music video. Retrieved from https://www.youtube.com/watch?v=IHyLiZTMmqg

4 Jackson, M. (2014, May 18). The art of dying Bruce Lee. Retrieved from https://www.youtube.com/watch?v=fWanEKIbfJk

5 Charlie Chaplin Official. (2016, March 10). Charlie Chaplin – Final speech from The Great Dictator. Retrieved from https://www.youtube.com/watch?v=J7GY1Xg6X20

6 Cassol, H., Pe´tre´, B., Degrange, S., Martial, C., Charland-Verville, V., Lallier, F., Bragard, I., Guillame, M., and Laureys, S. (2018). Qualitative thematic analysis of the phenomenology of near-death experiences. *PLoS ONE*, 13(2): e0193001. https://doi.org/10.1371/journal.pone.0193001

7 ABC News. (2018, April 15). Parents think boy is reincarnated pilot. Retrieved from https://abcnews.go.com/Primetime/story?id=132381&page=1

8 TEDx Talks. (2016, February 16). How to skip the small talk and connect with anyone / Kalina Silverman / TEDxWestministerCollege. Retrieved from https://www.youtube.com/watch?v=WDbxqM4Oy1Y&feature=youtu.be

BIBLIOGRAPHY

[9] Brennan, B. (1988). *Hands of light: A guide to healing through the human energy field.* Bantam Publishing.

[10] Tony Robbins. (2020, March 24). Retrieved from https://www.tonyrobbins.com/how-to-focus/

[11] A Tantric Life. (2018, August 9). A preview into the life & teachings of Shantam Nityama. Retrieved from https://www.youtube.com/watch?v=-2L_t72fRUI

[12] Csikszentmihalyi, M. (1990). *Flow: The psychology of optimal experience.* Harper Perennial.

[13] Csikszentmihalyi, M. (1990). *Flow: The psychology of optimal experience.* Harper Perennial.

[14] Graves, S. (2017). *Sacred orgasmic living.* Lulu Publishing.

[15] Einstein, A. (1954). *Ideas and Opinions.* Crown Publishers, Inc.

[16] FreeAgent. (2016, May 7). Vitvan – The Power to be Conscious. Retrieved from https://www.youtube.com/watch?v=AX4VAUIWvUE&list=WL&index=194

[17] Osho. (1974). *The book of secrets.* St. Martin's Griffin.

[18] Norbu, N. (1992). *Dream Yoga and the Practice of Natural Light.* Snow Lion Publications.

[19] Hubbard, G. S., May, E. C., and Puthoff, H. E. (released 2000). Possible production of photons during a remote viewing task: Preliminary results. *SRI International.* Retrieved from https://www.cia.gov/library/readingroom/docs/CIA-RDP96-00788R001800010002-1.pdf

[20] Putnam, F. W., Zahn, T. P., and Post, M. (1990). Differential autonomic nervous system activity in multiple personality disorder. *Psychiatry Research*, 31(3), pp. 251-260. https://doi.org/10.1016/0165-1781(90)90094-L

[21] Pearsall, P., Schwartz, G. E. R., and Russek, L. G. S. (2000). Changes in heart transplant recipients that parallel the personalities of their donors. *Integrative Medicine*, 2(2-3), pp. 65-72. https://doi.org/10.1016/S1096-2190(00)00013-5

[22] Pearsall, P., Schwartz, G. E. R., and Russek, L. G. S. (2000). Changes in heart transplant recipients that parallel the personalities of their donors. *Integrative Medicine*, 2(2-3), pp. 65-72. https://doi.org/10.1016/S1096-2190(00)00013-5

[23] History. (2010, October 1). Stan Lee's superhumans: Human calculator / history. Retrieved from https://www.youtube.com/watch?v=dtotrboSUqQ

[24] Great Big Story. (2016, December 13). Meet the accidental genius. Retrieved from https://www.youtube.com/watch?v=7H6doOmS-eM&feature=youtu.be

[25] Manufacturing Intellect., (2017, October 24). Savants and geniuses: A wonderful mystery documentary. Retrieved from https://www.youtube.com/watch?v=rTrJjbfG4xg&feature=youtu.be

[26] Kirsch, I. (2014). Antidepressants and the placebo effect. *Zeitschrift für Psychologie*, 222(3), pp. 128-134. https://doi.org/10.1027/2151-2604/a000176

[27] Wartolowska, K., Judge, A., Hopewell, S., Collins, G. S., Dean, B. J. F., Brindley, D., Savulescu, J., Beard, D., and Carr, A. J. (2014). Use of placebo controls in the evaluation of surgery: systematic review. *BMJ*, 348, g3253. https://doi.org/10.1136/bmj.g3253

BIBLIOGRAPHY

[28] Kirsch, I., Wampold, B., and Kelley, J. M. (2015). Controlling for the placebo effect in psychotherapy: Noble quest or tilting at windmills. *Psychology of Consciousness: Theory, Research, and Practice*. Advance online publication. https://doi.org/10.1037/cns0000065

[29] Whalley, B., and Hyland, M. (2013). Placebo by proxy: The effect of parents' beliefs on therapy for children's temper tantrums. *Journal of Behavior Medicine*, 36, pp. 341–346. https://doi.org/10.1007/s10865-012-9429-x

[30] Hagelin, J. S., Rainforth, M. V., Orme-Johnson, D. W., Cavanaugh, K. L., Alexander, C. N., Shatkin, S. F., Davies, J. L., Hughes, A. O., and Ross, E. (1999). Effects of group practice of the transcendental meditation program on preventing violent crime in Washington D. C.: Results of the national demonstration project, June-July 1993. *Social Indicators Research*, 47, pp. 153-201. Retrieved from http://www.gusp.org/pdf/Hagelin_1993_Natl_Demo_Proj.pdf

[31] Goldfinger Music. (2015, September 23). The last time. Retrieved from https://www.youtube.com/watch?v=Qo55-DZtwSE

[32] Van Gordon, W., Shonin, E., Dunn, T. J., Sapthiang, S., Kotera, Y., Garcia-Campayo, J., and Sheffield, D. (2018). Exploring emptiness and its effects on non-attachment, mystical experiences, and psycho-spiritual wellbeing: A quantitative and qualitative study of advanced meditators. *Explore: the Journal of Science and Healing*, pp. 1-34. https://doi.org/10.1016/j.explore.2018.12.003

[33] Naimy, M. (1988). *The Book of Mirdad*. Watkins Publishing.

[34] Johnlennon. (2010, August 24). Beautiful boy (darling boy). Retrieved from https://www.youtube.com/watch?v=Lt3IOdDE5iA

[35] Puiu, T. (2017, September 10). Your smartphone is millions of times more powerful than all of NASA's combined computing in 1969. Retrieved from https://www.zmescience.com/research/technology/smartphone-power-compared-to-apollo-432/

[36] Bostock, S., Crosswell, A. D., Prather, A. A., and Steptoe, A. (2018). Mindfulness on-the-go: Effects of a mindfulness meditation app on work stress and well-being. *Journal of Occupational Health Psychology*, Advance online publication, pp. 1-10. https://doi.org/10.1037/ocp0000118

[37] KRS One. (2009). *The Gospel of Hip Hop: The first instrument.* Powerhouse.

[38] N.A. (2018, July 29). Retrieved from Dictionary: https://www.google.com/search?biw=1679&bih=840&ei=YEoSW_PyK ISYsQXa57qYBQ&q=bored+definition&oq=bored+de&gs_l=psy-ab.1.0.0l10.3075.3864.0.4747.3.3.0.0.0.0.108.315.0j3.3.0....0...1.1.64.psy-ab..0.3.315...0i20i264k1j0i67k1j0i131k1.0.KbcF5-gSFe8

[39] HipHopIsInfinite. (2012, October 23). Learning, growing, changing. Retrieved from https://www.youtube.com/watch?v=ttHukW70TAM

[40] Ferriss, T. (2016). *Tools of Titans: The tactics, routines, and habits of billionaires, icons, and world-class performers.* Houghton Mifflin Harcourt.

[41] Goleansixsigma. (2020, February 22). Inspiration. Retrieved from https://goleansixsigma.com/think-can-think-cant-usually-right-confucius/

[42] Eckhart Tolle. (2019, February 8). How do I keep from being triggered? Retrieved from https://www.youtube.com/watch?v=lAaBXlC8-bU

[43] Marusak, H. A., Calhoun, V. D., Brown, S., Crespo, L. M., Sala-Hamrick, K., Gotlib, I. H., and Thomason, M. E. (2017). Dynamic function

connectivity of neurocognitive networks in children. *Human Brain Mapping*, 38(1), pp. 97-108. https://doi.org/10.1002/hbm.23346

[44] Osho. (2002). *Yoga. The science of breath.* St. Martin's Press.

[45] Burger, J. M. (2009). Replicating Milgram: Would people still obey today? *American Psychologist*, 64(1), pp. 1-11. https://doi.org/10.1037/a0010932

[46] McLeod, S. A. (2008). Zimbardo - Stanford Prison Experiment. Retrieved from http://www.simplypsychology.org/zimbardo.htm

[47] Damian Marley. (2011, March 23). Patience. Retrieved from https://www.youtube.com/watch?v=c9VQye6P8k0

[48] Gibson, E. (2019). *Race: The Root of All Evil (2nd ed.).* Independently Published.

[49] Feuerstein, G. (1998). *Tantra: The Path of Ecstasy.* Shambhala Publications, Inc.

[50] N. A. (2018, July 29). Quora. Retrieved from https://www.quora.com/How-many-types-of-calendars-are-in-the-world

[51] Timeanddate.com. (2018). The Chinese calendar. Retrieved from https://www.timeanddate.com/calendar/about-chinese.html

[52] Mad Lion. (2011, November 16). KRS-One Just Like That Official Video Prod. By MAD LION. Retrieved from https://www.youtube.com/watch?v=1q_C0o9GHsw

[53] Naimy, M. (1988). *The Book of Mirdad.* Watkins Publishing.

[54] Shatoosh. (2008, April 19). Michael Jordan 'maybe it's my fault' commercial. Retrieved from https://www.youtube.com/watch?v=9zSVu76AX3I

[55] Ferriss, T. (The Tim Ferriss Show). (2018, December 27). How to generate 8-figure revenue at age 21 (or any age) – real 4 -hour workweek case studies (#354).

[56] Eisenberger, N. I. (2014). An empirical review of the neural underpinnings of receiving and giving social support: Implications for health. *Psychosomatic Medicine*, 75(6), pp. 545-556. https://doi.org/10.1097/PSY.0b013e31829de2e7

[57] Goodreads. (2020). Charles Addams quotes. Retrieved from https://www.goodreads.com/author/quotes/52274.Charles_Addams

[58] Osho. (1974). *The book of secrets*. St. Martin's Griffin.

[59] Bastian, B., and Haslam, N. (2010). Excluded from humanity: The dehumanizing effects of social ostracism. *Journal of Experimental Social Psychology*, 46, pp. 107-113. https://doi.org/10.1016/j.jesp.2009.06.022

[60] Bastian, B., and Haslam, N. (2010). Excluded from humanity: The dehumanizing effects of social ostracism. *Journal of Experimental Social Psychology*, 46, pp. 107-113. https://doi.org/10.1016/j.jesp.2009.06.022

[61] Sunny Tooraw. (2009, April 20). George Carlin on drugs and marijuana. Retrieved from https://www.youtube.com/watch?v=oj5Sd3BRm_I

[62] Todd, R. M., Muller, D. J., Lee, D. H., Robertson, A., Eaton, T., Freeman, N., Palombo, D. J., Levine, B., and Anderson, A. K. (2013). Genes for emotion-enhanced remembering are linked to enhanced perceiving. Psychological Science, 24(11), pp. 2244-2253. https://doi.org/10.1177/0956797613492423

[63] Cutter, C. J., Schottenfeld, R. S., Moore, B. A., Ball, S. A., Beitel, M., Savant, J. D., Stults-Kolehmainen, M. A., Doucette, C., and Barry, D. T. (2014). A pilot trial of videogame-based exercise program for methadone

maintained patients. *Journal of Substance Abuse Treatments,* 47(4), pp. 209-305 https://doi.org/10.1016/j.jsat.2014.05.007

[64] Mermelstein, L. C., and Garske, J. P. (2015). A brief mindfulness intervention for college student binge drinkers: A pilot study. *Psychology of Addictive Behaviors,* 29(2), pp. 259-269. https://doi.org/10.1037/adb0000040

[65] Roughrider119. (2010, July 21). Bruce Lee "I do not hit" full complete scene. Retrieved from https://www.youtube.com/watch?v=hhvBTy28VJM

[66] Hurry, E. (2017). Medium. Retrieved from https://medium.com/@hurryemmanuel12/if-there-is-no-enemy-within-the-enemy-outside-can-do-us-no-harm-african-proverb-3d83ea282b6f

[67] Krippner, S. C. (2002). Conflicting perspectives on shamans and shamanism: Points and counterpoints. *American Psychologist,* 57(11), pp. 962-977. https://doi.org/10.1037/0003-066X.57.11.962

[68] Goodreads. (2019). Wim Hof quotes. Retrieved on November 1, 2019 from https://www.goodreads.com/author/quotes/5327058.Wim_Hof

[69] Nichols, H. (2017). The top 10 leading causes of death in the United States. Retrieved from https://www.medicalnewstoday.com/articles/282929.php

[70] Nichols, H. (2017). The top 10 leading causes of death in the United States. Retrieved from https://www.medicalnewstoday.com/articles/282929.php

[71] Nichols, H. (2017). The top 10 leading causes of death in the United States. Retrieved from https://www.medicalnewstoday.com/articles/282929.php

[72] Russell Brand. (2019, March 10). Heal yourself with The Ice Shaman / Wim Hof & Russell Brand. Retrieved from https://www.youtube.com/watch?v=JPPlicAEFec

[73] Goodreads. (2018). Quotable quote. Retrieved from https://www.goodreads.com/quotes/910217-absorb-what-is-useful-discard-what-is-useless-and-add

[74] Clifford, C. (2017, January 9). Tim Ferris: 3 things you should do every day if you want to be successful. Retrieved from https://www.cnbc.com/2017/01/09/tim-ferriss-reveals-his-top-3-must-have-daily-habits.html

[75] Sedlmeir, P., Eberth, J., Schwarz, M., Zimmermann, D., Haarig, F., Jaeger, S., and Kunze, S. (2012). The psychological effects of meditation: A meta-analysis. *Psychological Bulletin*, 138(6), pp. 1139-1171. https://doi.org/10.1037/a0028168

[76] Sedlmeir, P., Eberth, J., Schwarz, M., Zimmermann, D., Haarig, F., Jaeger, S., and Kunze, S. (2012). The psychological effects of meditation: A meta-analysis. *Psychological Bulletin*, 138(6), pp. 1139-1171. https://doi.org/10.1037/a0028168

[77] Greenberg, M. T., and Harris, A. R. (2012). Nurturing mindfulness in children and youth: Current state of research. *Child Development Perspectives*, 6(2), pp. 161–166. https://doi.org/10.1111/j.1750-8606.2011.00215.x

[78] Gotink, R. A., Meijboom, R., Vernooij, M. W., Smits, M., and Hunink, M. G. M. (2016). 8-week mindfulness based stress reduction induces brain changes similar to traditional long-term meditation practice – A systematic review. *Brain & Cognition*, 108, pp. 32-41. https://doi.org/10.1016/j.bandc.2016.07.001

BIBLIOGRAPHY

79 Navarro-Haro, M. V., Lopez-del-Hoyo, Y., Campos, D., Linehan, M. M., Hoffman, H. G., Garcia-Palacios, A., Modrego-Alacron, M., Borao, L., and Garcia-Campayo, J. (2017). Meditation experts try Virtual Reality mindfulness: A pilot study evaluation of the feasibility and acceptability of Virtual Reality to facilitate mindfulness practice in people attending a mindfulness conference. *PLoS ONE*, 12(11), e0187777. https://doi.org/10.1371/journal.pone.0187777

80 Shonin, E., Van Gordon, W., and Griffiths, D. (2014). Meditation awareness training (MAT) for improved psychological well-being: A qualitative examination of participant experiences. *Journal of Religion and Health*, 53(3), pp. 849 – 863. https://doi.org/10.1007/s10943-013-9679-0

81 Seppala, E. M., Nitschke, J. B., Tudorascu, D. L., Hayes, A., Goldstein, M. R., Nguyen, D. T. H., Perlman, D., and Davidson, R. J. (2014). Breathing-based meditation decreases posttraumatic stress disorder symptoms in U. S. military veterans: A randomized controlled longitudinal study. *Journal of Traumatic Stress*, 27, pp. 397-405. https://doi.org/10.1002/jts.21936

82 Brown, R. P., and Gerbarg, P. L. (2005). Sudarshan Kriya yogic breathing in the treatment of stress, anxiety, and depression: Part I – neurophysiologic model. *The Journal of Alternative and Complementary Medicine*, 11(1), pp. 189-201. https://doi.org/10.1089/acm.2005.11.189

83 Seppala, E. M., Nitschke, J. B., Tudorascu, D. L., Hayes, A., Goldstein, M. R., Nguyen, D. T. H., Perlman, D., and Davidson, R. J. (2014). Breathing-based meditation decreases posttraumatic stress disorder symptoms in U. S. military veterans: A randomized controlled longitudinal study. *Journal of Traumatic Stress*, 27, pp. 397-405. https://doi.org/10.1002/jts.21936

[84] Seppala, E. M., Nitschke, J. B., Tudorascu, D. L., Hayes, A., Goldstein, M. R., Nguyen, D. T. H., Perlman, D., and Davidson, R. J. (2014). Breathing-based meditation decreases posttraumatic stress disorder symptoms in U. S. military veterans: A randomized controlled longitudinal study. *Journal of Traumatic Stress*, 27, pp. 397-405. https://doi.org/10.1002/jts.21936

[85] Qi Gong Institute. (2018). Understanding meditation. Retrieved on June 11, 2018 from https://qigonginstitute.org/category/18/meditation

[86] Field, T. (2009). *Tai Chi and Chi Gong.* American Psychological Association

[87] Ripley's Believe It or Not. (2018, April 16). How Shaolin Monks obtain their superpowers. Retrieved from https://www.ripleys.com/weird-news/shaolin-monks/

[88] DDP Yoga. (2012, April 30). Never, ever give up. Arthur's inspirational transformation. Retrieved from https://www.youtube.com/watch?v=qX9FSZJu448

[89] Osho Quotes. (2020, February 26). Osho quotes on sex. Retrieved from https://www.osho.com/highlights-of-oshos-world/osho-on-sex-quotes

[90] Osho International. (2012, December 6). Osho: Sex is your life force. Retrieved from https://www.youtube.com/watch?v=KmThdVnWNi8

[91] A Tantric Life. (2018, August 9). A preview into the life & teachings of Shantam Nityama. Retrieved from https://www.youtube.com/watch?v=-2L_t72fRUI

[92] A Tantric Life. (2018, August 9). A preview into the life & teachings of Shantam Nityama. Retrieved from https://www.youtube.com/watch?v=-2L_t72fRUI

BIBLIOGRAPHY

[93] Osho International Foundation. (2019, August 15). The Navel Seat of Will. Retrieved from https://www.osho.com/osho-online-library/osho-talks/meditation-asleep-wake-up-06d1eae4-434?p=e43b004c4480ad0bab7b40474e02efc4

[94] Remedies Health Communities. (2018, August 15). Sleep disorders. Retrieved from http://www.healthcommunities.com/sleep-disorders/overview-of-sleep-disorders.shtml

[95] The Atlantic. (2018, August 15). Americans are getting worse at taking sleeping pills. Retrieved from https://www.theatlantic.com/health/archive/2014/08/americans-are-getting-worse-at-taking-sleeping-pills/375935/

[96] The Atlantic. (2018, August 15). Americans are getting worse at taking sleeping pills. Retrieved from https://www.theatlantic.com/health/archive/2014/08/americans-are-getting-worse-at-taking-sleeping-pills/375935/

[97] Hill, N. (1987). *Think and Grow Rich*. Fawcett Books.

[98] AZ Quotes. (2019). Paramahansa Yogananda quotes. Retrieved on October 30, 2019 from https://www.azquotes.com/quote/702776

[99] Mfvn. (2018, July 12). Joe Rogan on shoulder stretching. Retrieved from https://www.youtube.com/watch?v=KfOoRJIN1V8

[100] Brainy Quote. (2020). Arnold Schwarzenegger quotes. Retrieved on January 20, 2020 from https://www.brainyquote.com/quotes/arnold_schwarzenegger_146582

[101] Hsueh, M. F., Önnerfjord, P., Bolognesi, M. P., Easley, M. E., and Kraus, V. B. (2019). Analysis of "old" proteins unmasks dynamic gradient

of cartilage turnover in human limbs. *Science Advances*, 5(10). https://doi.org/10.1126/sciadv.aax3203

[102] Athlean-X. (2016, December 8). Muscle building diet mistake (eat big / get big!). Retrieved from https://www.youtube.com/watch?v=-CHmorGmjmg

[103] National Institute of Diabetes and Digestive and Kidney Diseases. (2018, August 26). Overweight & obesity statistics. Retrieved from https://www.niddk.nih.gov/health-information/health-statistics/overweight-obesity

[104] Harvard Health Publishing. (2017, April 11). Why people become overweight. Retrieved from https://www.health.harvard.edu/staying-healthy/why-people-become-overweight

[105] Schwalfenberg, G. (2012). The alkaline diet: Is there evidence that an alkaline pH diet benefits health? *Journal of Environmental and Public Health*, Article ID 727630. https://doi.org/10.1155/2012/727630

[106] Djfatdex. (2011, June 29). Healthy livin' by Stic – The workout. Retrieved from https://www.youtube.com/watch?v=SsTffAB9Dvo

[107] Pinterest. (2019). Dr. Sebi's cell food. Retrieved on October 17, 2019 from https://www.pinterest.com/pin/353603008239166638/?nic=1

[108] Radin, D., Lund, N., Emoto, M., and Kizu, T. (2008). Effects of distant intention on water crystal formation: A triple-blind replication. *Journal of Scientific Replication*, 00(0). Retrieved from http://www.deanradin.com/papers/emotoIIproof.pdf

[109] Emoto, M. (2016). *The Secrets of Water: For the Children of the World*. Beyond Words Publishing, Inc.

BIBLIOGRAPHY

[110] Radin, D., Lund, N., Emoto, M., and Kizu, T. (2008). Effects of distant intention on water crystal formation: A triple-blind replication. *Journal of Scientific Replication*, 00(0). Retrieved from http://www.deanradin.com/papers/emotoIIproof.pdf

[111] Longo, V. D., and Panda, S. (2017). Fasting, circadian rhythms, and time restricted feeding in healthy lifespan. *Cell Metabolism*, 23(6), pp. 1048-1059. https://doi.org/10.1016/j.cmet.2016.06.001

[112] Dorian Wilson. (2019, June 29). Water fasting: The complete guide (fastest fat loss method). Retrieved from https://www.youtube.com/watch?v=DghrZNUP5vo

[113] Osho. (2018, August 26). Go slow on the fast! Retrieved from https://www.osho.com/read/featured-books/yoga/go-slow-on-that-fast

[114] Osho. (2018, August 26). Go slow on the fast! Retrieved from https://www.osho.com/read/featured-books/yoga/go-slow-on-that-fast

[115] Osborne, H. (2017, May 11). Exercise has anti-aging benefits and makes you years younger on a cellular level. Retrieved from https://www.newsweek.com/exercise-anti-aging-younger-cellular-level-telomeres-607228

[116] Athlean-X. (2016, July 28). Weightlifting belts. Weak abs (uh-oh!!!). Retrieved from https://www.youtube.com/watch?v=aBgv30fkD7c

[117] Foundmyfitness. (2017, June 15). Dr. Jari Laukkanen on sauna use for the prevention of cardiovascular & alzheimer's disease. Retrieved from https://www.youtube.com/watch?v=jL7vVG_CFWA

[118] EverydayPower. (2019). 40 Nipsey Hussle quotes celebrating his life and music. Retrieved on October 17, 2019 from https://everydaypower.com/nipsey-hussle-quotes/

[119] AZ Quotes. (2018, August 26). George Carlin quotes about laughter. Retrieved from https://www.azquotes.com/author/2470-George_Carlin/tag/laughter

[120] Edgar Cayce Arizona A. R. E. (2019, June 14). Edgar Cayce on Humor. Retrieved from https://www.youtube.com/watch?v=byfY7qItDvE&feature=youtu.be

[121] McGraw, P., and Warner, J. (2018). Meet the people who use humor to heal. *Psychology Today*. Retrieved on June 10, 2018 from https://www.psychologytoday.com/us/blog/the-humor-code/201206/meet-the-people-who-use-humor-heal

[122] Kosterich, J. (2017, July 9). The benefits of laughing. Retrieved from http://slowaging.org/benefits-of-laughing/

[123] Goodreads. (2018, August 26). John Muir quotes. Retrieved from https://www.goodreads.com/author/quotes/5297.John_Muir

[124] Business Insider. (2016, April 22). 11 scientific reasons you should be spending more time outside. Retrieved from https://www.businessinsider.com/scientific-benefits-of-nature-outdoors-2016-4

[125] Live Strong. (2017, September 11). What are the health benefits of swimming in sea water? Retrieved from https://www.livestrong.com/article/158987-what-are-the-benefits-of-salt-scrubs/

[126] Huffington Post. (2016, April 30). Connecting with nature has real health benefits. Retrieved from https://www.huffingtonpost.ca/davidsuzukifoundation/nature-health_b_9801764.html

BIBLIOGRAPHY

[127] Mother Nature Network. (2013, November 5). Seven deserts that used to be verdant fields and forests. Retrieved from https://www.mnn.com/earth-matters/wilderness-resources/blogs/7-deserts-that-used-to-be-verdant-fields-and-forests

[128] John of God. (2018, November 12). John of God - João de Deus. The Miracle Man of Brazil. Retrieved from https://johnofgod.com/

[129] Baughman, K. R., Burke, R. C., Hewit, M. S., Sudano, J. J., Meeker, J., and Hull, S. K. (2015). Associations between difficulty paying medical bills and forgone medical and prescription drug care. *Population Health Management*, 18(5), pp. 358-366. https://doi.org/10.1089/pop.2014.0128

[130] Walgate, R. (2009). European health systems face scrutiny in US debate. *The Lancet*, 374(9699), pp. 1407-1408. https://doi.org/10.1016/S0140-6736(09)61845-6

[131] Goalcast. (2018, July 6). How bamboo trees will bring out your best self / Les Brown / Goalcast. Retrieved from https://www.youtube.com/watch?v=gMWXMMUg5pI

[132] MrChildhood99. (2011, May 10). Public Enemy he got game. Retrieved from https://www.youtube.com/watch?v=F5d5omWxFJk

[133] Emmons, R. A., and Stern, R. (2013). Gratitude as a psychotherapeutic intervention. *Journal of Clinical Psychology: In Session*, 69(8), pp. 846-855. https://doi.org/10.1002/jclp.22020

[134] Lewis Howes. (2014, November 24). Tony Robbins 7 simple steps to financial freedom - Lewis Howes. Retrieved from https://www.youtube.com/watch?v=kSoO2KjVVG4

[135] Johnlennon. (2016, December 18). Instant Karma! (We all shine on) – Lennon/Ono with the Plastic Ono Band. Retrieved from https://www.youtube.com/watch?v=xLy2SaSQAtA

[136] Movieclips. (2015, January 2). Unforgiven (7/10) movie clip – We all have it coming (1992). Retrieved from https://www.youtube.com/watch?v=cAYVS8aRQ1U

[137] Osho. (1974). *The book of secrets*. St. Martin's Griffin.

[138] BobMarley. (2017, May 14). Bob Marley – Redemption Song. Retrieved from https://www.youtube.com/watch?v=Md8EesTaIsA

[139] Fuad Hariz. (2012, February 14). Tyler Durden philosophy of life – fight club. Retrieved from https://www.youtube.com/watch?v=CWRTqMGvdpc

[140] A Tantric Life. (2018, August 9). A preview into the life & teachings of Shantam Nityama. Retrieved from https://www.youtube.com/watch?v=-2L_t72fRUI

[141] Heart to Heart with Shakti Sundari. (2017, March 5). Shantam Nityama – The Tantric Mongoose – heart to heart with Shakti Sundari. Retrieved from https://www.youtube.com/watch?v=sKXCnlv7PAY&t=2058s

[142] Osho. (2018, August 28). No beginning. No end. Retrieved from https://www.osho.com/iosho/library/read-book/online-library-joshu-queen-elizabeth-different-cdd2c845-1a7?p=9d3ede5d84af6e1ec3076488f03e66d1

[143] Philosophy Now. (2014). Plato's ideal ruler today. Retrieved on November 3, 2019 from https://philosophynow.org/issues/101/Platos_Ideal_Ruler_Today

BIBLIOGRAPHY

144 Discover Magazine. (2009, December 23). #73: Yes, you really can smell fear. Retrieved from http://discovermagazine.com/2010/jan-feb/075

145 USA Today. (2016, January 12). Teen girl uses 'crazy strength' to lift burning car off dad. Retrieved from https://www.usatoday.com/story/news/humankind/2016/01/12/teen-girl-uses-crazy-strength-lift-burning-car-off-dad/78675898/

146 Jeffrey, S. (2014, February 26). A complete guide to self-actualization: 5 key steps to accelerate growth. https://scottjeffrey.com/self-actualization/

147 RR Web Designer. (2017, February 7). Napoleon Hill – 17 Principles (1 of 6). Retrieved from https://www.youtube.com/watch?v=ZpPhpBQfiJY

148 Deckdisk. (2009, May 12). Ziggy Marley – Love is my religion. Retrieved from https://www.youtube.com/watch?v=r-eXYJnV3V4

149 Nick Cannon. (2019, March 29). [Full Session] Cannon's Class with KRS ONE. Retrieved from https://youtu.be/wcxroujFPN0

150 AZ Quotes. (2020, February 5). AZ Quotes. Retrieved from https://www.azquotes.com/quote/597315

151 Word Porn. (2018, April 11). Here's why you're wasting your life / Muhammad Ali. Retrieved from https://www.youtube.com/watch?v=-Ab3tQ_6P4E

152 London Real. (2019, September 18). Dr. Joe Dispenza – How not to be controlled by the environment / London Real. Retrieved from https://www.youtube.com/watch?v=29QIOpAAKjM&feature=youtu.be

[153] Piotrekzprod. (2018, October 9). The Mind of Kobe Bryant – Confidence. Retrieved from https://www.youtube.com/watch?v=iXciUuVQvTc&feature=youtu.be

[154] Csikszentmihalyi, M. (1990). *Flow: The psychology of optimal experience.* Harper Perennial.

[155] Csikszentmihalyi, M. (1990). *Flow: The psychology of optimal experience.* Harper Perennial.

[156] Brainyquote. (2018, November 20). Bruce Lee quotes. Retrieved from https://www.brainyquote.com/quotes/bruce_lee_413509

[157] Moore, B. A. (2013). Propensity for experiencing flow: The roles of cognitive flexibility and mindfulness. *The Humanistic Psychologist*, 41(4), pp. 319-332. https://doi.org/10.1080/08873267.2013.820954

[158] Van Gordon, W., Shonin, E., Dunn, T. J., Sapthiang, S., Kotera, Y., Garcia-Campayo, J., and Sheffield, D. (2018). Exploring emptiness and its effects on non-attachment, mystical experiences, and psycho-spiritual wellbeing: A quantitative and qualitative study of advanced meditators. *Explore: the Journal of Science and Healing*, pp. 1-34. https://doi.org/10.1016/j.explore.2018.12.003

[159] Moore, B. A. (2013). Propensity for experiencing flow: The roles of cognitive flexibility and mindfulness. *The Humanistic Psychologist*, 41(4), pp. 319-332. https://doi.org/10.1080/08873267.2013.820954

[160] Wonder Jam. (2014, June 13). Jim Carrey – Inspiring commencement speech Maharishi University. Retrieved from https://www.youtube.com/watch?v=q2rVDCrt6QY

BIBLIOGRAPHY

161 Huffpost. (2013, August 3). The top five regrets of the dying. Retrieved on October 20, 2019 from https://www.huffpost.com/entry/top-5-regrets-of-the-dying_n_3640593

162 Visual Complexity. (2009, January 27). Brain + Universe. Retrieved on October 20, 2019 from http://www.visualcomplexity.com/vc/blog/?p=234

163 A Tantric Life. (2018, August 9). A preview into the life & teachings of Shantam Nityama. Retrieved from https://www.youtube.com/watch?v=-2L_t72fRUI

164 Thrive Global. (2017, February 11). Breathe. Retrieved on October 21, 2019 from https://medium.com/thrive-global/breathe-5749aeb9f4f0

165 Osho. (2002). *Yoga: The science of breath*. St. Martin's Press.

166 Eat Squat Cum. (2019, January 16). The most basic tool to enhance your sex life. Retrieved from https://youtu.be/R1y6C8SeMnY

167 Osho. (1974). *The book of secrets*. St. Martin's Griffin.

168 Hof, W. (2015). The ice man. Retrieved from http://www.icemanwimhof.com/en-home

169 Powerful JRE. (2015, October 25). Joe Rogan breathing with "the Iceman" Wim Hof (from Joe Rogan experience #712). Retrieved from https://www.youtube.com/watch?v=A9zS94x2nd8

170 Muzik, O., Reilly, K. T., and Diwadkar, V. A. (2018). "Brain over body"–A study on the willful regulation of autonomic function during cold exposure. *NeuroImage*, 172, pp. 632-641. https://doi.org/10.1016/j.neuroimage.2018.01.067

[171] Kox, M., van Eijk, L. T., Zwaag, J., van den Wildenberg, J., Sweep, F. C. G. J., van der Hoeven, J. G., and Pickkers, P. (2014). Voluntary activation of the sympathetic nervous system and attenuation of the innate immune response in humans. *Proceedings of the National Academy of the Sciences of the United States of America*, 111(20), pp. 7379-7384. https://doi.org/10.1073/pnas.1322174111

[172] Powerful JRE. (2015, October 25). Joe Rogan breathing with "the Iceman" Wim Hof (from Joe Rogan experience #712). Retrieved from https://www.youtube.com/watch?v=A9zS94x2nd8

[173] Osho. (1974). *The book of secrets*. St. Martin's Griffin.

[174] School of the Natural Order of Colorado. (2018, February 14). How to see and think of this world as an energy world. Retrieved from https://www.youtube.com/watch?v=FHZexlfZois&list=PLNnayPqy4uf S8Y1ZkUcTR6i9NKjR2NnxD&index=49&t=0s

[175] CarbonNation TV. (2016, January 31). KRS One 5th dimension explained. Retrieved from https://www.youtube.com/watch?v=_Ss6i7uUPwA

[176] Van Gordon, W., Shonin, E., Dunn, T. J., Sapthiang, S., Kotera, Y., Garcia-Campayo, J., and Sheffield, D. (2018). Exploring emptiness and its effects on non-attachment, mystical experiences, and psycho-spiritual wellbeing: A quantitative and qualitative study of advanced meditators. *Explore: the Journal of Science and Healing*, pp. 1-34. https://doi.org/10.1016/j.explore.2018.12.003

[177] Jackson, M. (2014, May 18). The art of dying Bruce Lee. Retrieved from https://www.youtube.com/watch?v=fWanEKIbfJk

[178] Van Gordon, W., Shonin, E., Dunn, T. J., Sapthiang, S., Kotera, Y., Garcia-Campayo, J., and Sheffield, D. (2018). Exploring emptiness and its

effects on non-attachment, mystical experiences, and psycho-spiritual wellbeing: A quantitative and qualitative study of advanced meditators. *Explore: the Journal of Science and Healing*, pp. 1-34. https://doi.org/10.1016/j.explore.2018.12.003

[179] Winfield, C. (2016, February 23). 5 morning rituals that help you 'win the day'. Retrieved from https://www.inc.com/chris-winfield/5-morning-rituals-that-help-you-win-the-day-.html

[180] Shannon, G., McKenna, M. F., Angeloni, L. M., Crooks, K. R., Fristrup, K. M., Brown, E., Warner, K. A., Nelson, M. D., White, C., Briggs, J., McFarland, S., and Wittemyer, G. (2016). A synthesis of two decades of research documenting the effects of noise on wildlife. *Biological Reviews*, 91, pp. 982-1005 https://doi.org/10.1111/brv.12207

[181] Pace, W. R. (1962). Oral communication and sales effectiveness. *Journal of Applied Psychology*, 46(5), pp. 321-324. https://doi.org/10.1037/h0043815

[182] Merriam-Webster. (2018, August 17). Dictionary. Retrieved from https://www.merriam-webster.com/dictionary/dialogue

[183] Hof, W. (2019). Wim Hof Method. Retrieved from https://www.wimhofmethod.com/

[184] Medical Daily. (2014, June 24). Benefits of cold showers: 7 reasons why taking cold showers is good for your health. Retrieved from https://www.medicaldaily.com/benefits-cold-showers-7-reasons-why-taking-cool-showers-good-your-health-289524

[185] The Art of Manliness. (2010, January 18). The James Bond shower: A shot of cold water for health and vitality. Retrieved from https://www.artofmanliness.com/articles/the-james-bond-shower-a-shot-of-cold-water-for-health-and-vitality/

[186] Osho. (1974). *The book of secrets*. St. Martin's Griffin.

[187] A Tantric Life. (2017, June 12). Shantam Nityama – the body never lies. Retrieved from https://www.youtube.com/watch?v=MbA6TahyR4k

[188] Bruce Lipton. (2019, May 20). What are the volts of electricity in your human body. Retrieved on October 21, 2019 from https://www.brucelipton.com/blog/what-are-the-volts-electricity-your-human-body

[189] Posadzki, P. (2010). The psychology of Qi Gong: A qualitative study. *Complementary Health Practice Review*, 15(2), pp. 84-97. https://doi.org/10.1177/1533210110387019

[190] OWN. (2012, November 11). Eckhart Tolle Reveals how to silence voices in your head / SuperSoul Sunday / Oprah Winfrey Network. Retrieved from https://www.youtube.com/watch?v=QnZ83CSVWF8

[191] Graves, S. (2017). *Sacred orgasmic living*. Lulu Publishing.

[192] Osho Plus. (2017, June 5). Best life changing quotes of all time. Retrieved from http://oshoplus.blogspot.com/2017/06/osho-quotes-on-sex-best-quotes-on-sex.html

[193] A Tantric Life. (2018, August 9). A preview into the life & teachings of Shantam Nityama. Retrieved from https://www.youtube.com/watch?v=-2L_t72fRUI

[194] Graves, S. (2017). *Sacred orgasmic living*. Lulu Publishing.

[195] A Tantric Life. (2018, August 9). A preview into the life & teachings of Shantam Nityama. Retrieved from https://www.youtube.com/watch?v=-2L_t72fRUI

BIBLIOGRAPHY

[196] Fiz1432. (2008, August 3). Shantam Nityama – Tantric Mongoose pt. 1. Retrieved from https://www.youtube.com/watch?v=8bubJFPQHYE

[197] BBC News. (2013, July 5). Why deaf people sneeze silently. Retrieved from https://www.bbc.com/news/blogs-ouch-23162903

[198] Roughrider119. (2010, July 21). Bruce Lee "I do not hit" full complete scene. Retrieved from https://www.youtube.com/watch?v=hhvBTy28VJM

[199] Jackson, M. (2014, May 18). The art of dying Bruce Lee. Retrieved from https://www.youtube.com/watch?v=fWanEKIbfJk

Chad offers the following services:

Live Seminars:

Each transformational seminar is specifically developed to meet the needs of your school or organization.

Instruction is available in the following areas of interest:

Mindfulness/meditation, optimal performance, accessing the flow state, human sexuality, Tantra, community building, creating life satisfaction, team building, and nonprofit management.

Individual coaching is also available in the aforementioned subject matter.

Energy Bodywork:

Energy Bodywork utilizes Life Force Energy (Kundalini) to connect to the core of our being. This may be pleasurable for some, and cathartic for others. This depends on what is needed for the moment. Every session is different, as we are constantly evolving beings. This work is discussed in greater detail on his website, and in the chapter "Vessels for Healing".

To contact Chad please visit: **OneLoveHolisticHealth.com**

CPSIA information can be obtained
at www.ICGtesting.com
Printed in the USA
LVHW050510011221
704868LV00012B/1256